FIRST RATE SHIP.

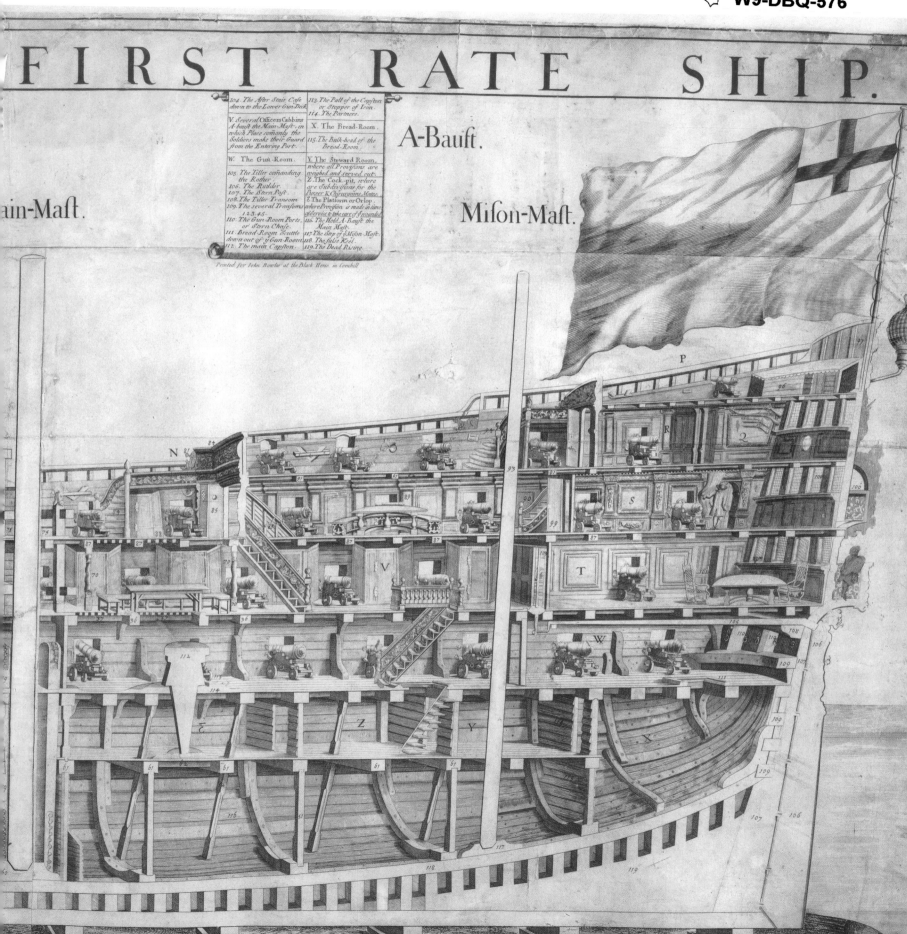

A-Bauft.

Main-Maft.

Mifon-Maft.

104. The After Stair Cafe down to the Lower Gun Deck	113. The Pall of the Capston or Stopper of Iron.
V. Several Officers Cabbins A-bauft the Main-Maft, in which Place comonly the Soldiers make their Guard from the Entering Port.	114. The Partners.
	X. The Bread-Room.
	115. The Bulk-head of the Bread-Room.
W. The Gun-Room.	Y. The Steward Room, where all Provisions are weighed and served out.
105. The Tiller comanding the Rother	Z. The Cock-pit, where are Subdivisions for the Purser & Chirurgeons Mates.
106. The Rudder.	&. The Platform or Orlop, where Provision is made in time of service to take care of y wounded.
107. The Stern Post.	116. The Hold, A-Bauft the Main Maft.
108. The Tiller Transom	117. The step of y Mifon-Maft.
109. The several Transoms 1.2.3.4.5.	118. The false Keel.
110. The Gun-Room Ports or Stern Chafe.	119. The Dead Rising.
111. Bread-Room Scuttle down out of y Gun-Room	
112. The main Capston.	

Printed for John Bowles at the Black Horse in Cornhill

HEART *of* OAK

A Sailor's Life in Nelson's Navy

HEART of OAK

A Sailor's Life in Nelson's Navy

JAMES P. McGUANE

W. W. NORTON & COMPANY

New York · London

To Brigid, with love

For information about permission to reproduce
selections from this book, write to Permissions,
W. W. Norton & Company, Inc.,
500 Fifth Avenue, New York, NY 10110.

The text of this book is composed in Cochin Roman
with the display set in Cochin Bold Italic.
Manufacturing by South China Printing, Ltd.
Book design by Kavanagh Design/NY
Author's photograph: Karl Peiler
Production manager: Andrew Marasia

Endpapers: From an anonymous copper engraving
published in the mid-eighteenth century. It depicts
the skeleton of a "first rate" ship of the line. The
vessel would be from a slightly earlier period evidenced
by the "whipstaff" steering mechanism which was in
use before the adoption of the steering wheel. From the
collection of Mr. Anthony Cross, Warwick Leadlay
Gallery, 5 Nelson Road, Greenwich, London, SE10
9JB, UK.

ISBN 0-393-04749-0

W. W. Norton & Company, Inc.
500 Fifth Avenue, New York N.Y. 10110
www.wwnorton.com

W. W. Norton & Company Ltd.
Castle House, 75/76 Wells Street,
London WIT 3QT

1 2 3 4 5 6 7 8 9 0

CONTENTS

Introduction

NELSON'S NAVY

Using the span of Horatio Nelson's life and career as a reference, we look at Nelson's navy. His years also nicely coincide with England's other struggle, with the rebellious colonies in America. By closely examining the objects that "Jack Tar" used, we hope to know him better.

Nelson's victory at Trafalgar established England as the dominant sea power for generations to come. The age of fighting sail would soon change. The steam engine, exploding shells and armor cladding were to become the new technology in naval warfare.

HMS *Invincible*, above
HMS *Victory*, opposite

HMS INVINCIBLE

The documentary search for objects from the Nelson era inevitably led me to the Chatham Historic Dockyard. It was from this Royal Naval dockyard that Nelson's Trafalgar flagship HMS *Victory* was launched in 1765.

There is an ever-growing display at the Dockyard Museum of artifacts recovered from the HMS *Invincible*. I am grateful that I was granted access to the museum's collections.

The HMS *Invincible*, a 74-gun ship-of-the-line, sank after running aground (with no loss of life) in 1758. (Coincidentally, 1758 is the year that Horatio Nelson was born). Only after the wreck site in the East Solent, off Southampton, had been carefully surveyed in the 1980s did the recovery and preservation of artifacts begin. The very important relationship between the objects themselves and their former location aboard ship has been faithfully recorded.

The conservation and restoration of such materials as metal, wood, cloth and leather has been carried out with great care. The oxygen-free composition of the mud and silt at the site has miraculously spared fragile objects from decay for well over 200 years. These same items (even a cannonball) can quickly decompose after they are brought to the surface unless prompt scientific intervention takes place. A wooden object, unrecognizable to all but the trained eye, appears as a dark, spongy, congealed mass with the consistency of wet papier-maché. With care, it can be slowly coaxed to return to its original shape and rigidity even down to scratches, carvings, nicks and abrasions. As the recovery, restoration and interpretation of these objects continues to unfold, our understanding of naval life becomes richer.

HMS *Invincible* was notable for several reasons. She was built by the French in 1744 and captured by the English in 1747. The ship was re-rigged to suit the Royal Navy and commissioned as HMS *Invincible*. Her speed, design and sailing qualities were such that her lines were quickly and carefully duplicated. It's a tribute to her French designers that her hull speed and firepower influenced the admiralty for decades.

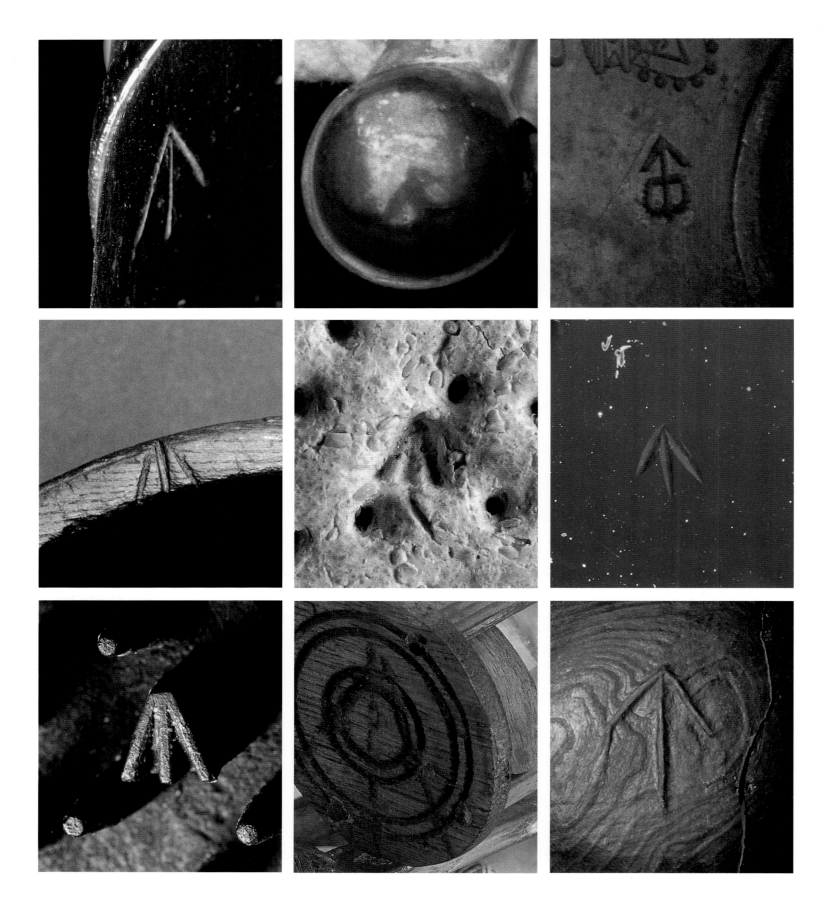

THE BROAD ARROW

The photographic details on the left should serve as examples of the "broad arrow." Simply stated, the broad arrow is a brand that identifies an object as government property. As property of the Crown, it would be a criminal offense to possess it. The identification was not peculiar to the Royal Navy. It was a universal statement of ownership by the British government: "Property of His Majesty the King." It was scribed, scratched, stamped, printed, painted, carved, etched, branded or otherwise affixed or attached to virtually everything. We find it on guns, tools, clothing, utensils, leather goods, glass, wood, metal and cloth. It must have been somewhat of a deterrent against theft. The value of contraband would certainly have been diminished since the goods would clearly state: Stolen from the King.

When items were ordered from craftsmen for use in His Majesty's Service, the purchase agreement would require that the objects all be supplied with the mark. If items were fashioned from raw materials as, for instance, aboard ship, a simpler, often cruder, arrow was affixed. The use of the mark sometimes disrespectfully called "the crow's foot" is recorded back to the time of the Crusades.

The mark is useful to the archaeologist and the historian in determining what might be an individual's private property and what clearly is not. A cannon, for instance, that was clearly manufactured in France might be marked with the broad arrow after being seized as a prize of war and put into service by the British.

❖ ❖ ❖

GRATEFUL ACKNOWLEDGMENT

I wish to add a special thanks to the many people who helped me with this book. I feel privileged that I was trusted with delicate and irreplaceable objects from Britain's past. The museums, libraries, ships, collectors, curators, military personnel, archaeologists and other experts who aided me have my sincere appreciation. Simon Bernard and Tony Corbell of Hasselblad Camera and Kodak Professional provided valuable technical help. At the risk of failing to mention other important contributors, I would like to note the following individuals:

Peter Goodwin, Keeper, HMS *Victory*; Lt. Kerry Straughan, Executive Officer, HMS *Victory*; Brian Lavery, National Maritime Museum; Richard Holdsworth and Bruce Robertson, The Chatham Historic Dockyard Trust; Chief Petty Officer Nigel Goddard, Curator, Plymouth Naval Base Museum; Pieter van der Merwe, The National Maritime Museum; Captain George Hogg, RN, Ret., Falmouth Maritime Museum; Joan Davis, Padstow Shipwreck Museum; Anthony Cross, Warwick-Leadlay Galleries, Greenwich; Colin White, The Royal Naval Museum; Fergus Waters, Hartlepool Historic Quay; Brian Hopkins HMS *Trincomalee* Trust; Susan Lindsay, Royal Marines Museum; Alex Jastrzebski, Chatham Historic Dockyard, Conservation Laboratory; Dave Elliott, Sailmaker, Sail and Color's Loft, Chatham Historic Dockyard; Beverley Burford, Greenwich Borough Museum; Michael Maud, The Rochester Guildhall Museum; Tony Pearce, Morris Maritime Museum, Penzance; Michael Phillips, Historian, Saltash, Cornwall; and Starling Lawrence, W. W. Norton & Company.

Nelson and HMS Victory

LARGE SHIP MODEL
Chatham Historic Dockyard Museum, Chatham, Kent
7.5 meters long

The Chatham Yard has recently acquired a 7.5-meter-long (25 ft.) scale model of Nelson's HMS *Victory*. Hollywood built the ship as a special effects prop for a 1941 motion picture starring Laurence Olivier and Vivien Leigh. The film was released in Europe with the title *Lady Hamilton*. The American release was titled *That Hamilton Woman!*

Two people can fit in special hatches on the deck. It is currently being prepared for exhibit in the same yard that built the original HMS *Victory*.

GRAVE of WALTER BURKE
Wouldham, Kent
120cm. tall

The grave of purser Walter Burke in the churchyard at Wouldham, not far from Chatham. He lived for ten years after Trafalgar, and would have been about sixty at the time he held the dying Nelson.

BRONZE PARKER PLAQUE
Cemetery in Deal, Kent
35cm. wide

"This is the Tomb of Captain Edward Thornborough Parker, a gallant and distinguished Commander who wounded in action off Boulogne, died on 27 September 1801, aged 23 years. Admiral Lord Nelson, whose friend he was attended his funeral."

It is know that Admiral Nelson doted on the young mortally wounded captain and visited him daily when possible. Nelson was about twenty years his senior.

"VICTORY" CHAIR

Phillips Auctioneers, New York, New York
94cm. high. Oak with leather cushion.

This Regency armchair was reputedly made for Prime Minister William Pitt the Younger. Pitt, however, died in the spring of 1806, just a half year after Trafalgar, and the chair is likely to have been presented to Pitt's elder brother, John, 2nd Earl of Chatham.

The oak was stripped from HMS *Victory* during her repair at Chatham. The piece is signed by its maker, Lionel Abington. It is carved with the name "Victory," "Trafalgar," the Royal Coat of Arms and Nelson's insignia, with a star, snake and staff. The arm terminals are modeled as cannons, 24 pounders. Additional carved details show oak leaves, acorns, serpents, ship's rudder, gunnery tools, laurel wreaths and palm leaves. The chair features a caned seat and morocco leather cushion. It was in Pitt's family's possession until it was sold at auction in London in 1997 for over £38,000.

SAIL FRAGMENT, *opposite*

Rochester Guildhall Museum, Rochester, Kent
155mm. wide, 120mm. high

"89 holes. Part of the Maintopsail of HMS *Victory* bent before fighting the Battle of Trafalgar."

The sailors put forth the effort of counting the shot holes in one of HMS *Victory's* battle-tattered sails before painting the inscription on the small scrap. Aside from being a chilling reminder of the fierce battle, it provides us with a close-up view of Royal Navy canvas.

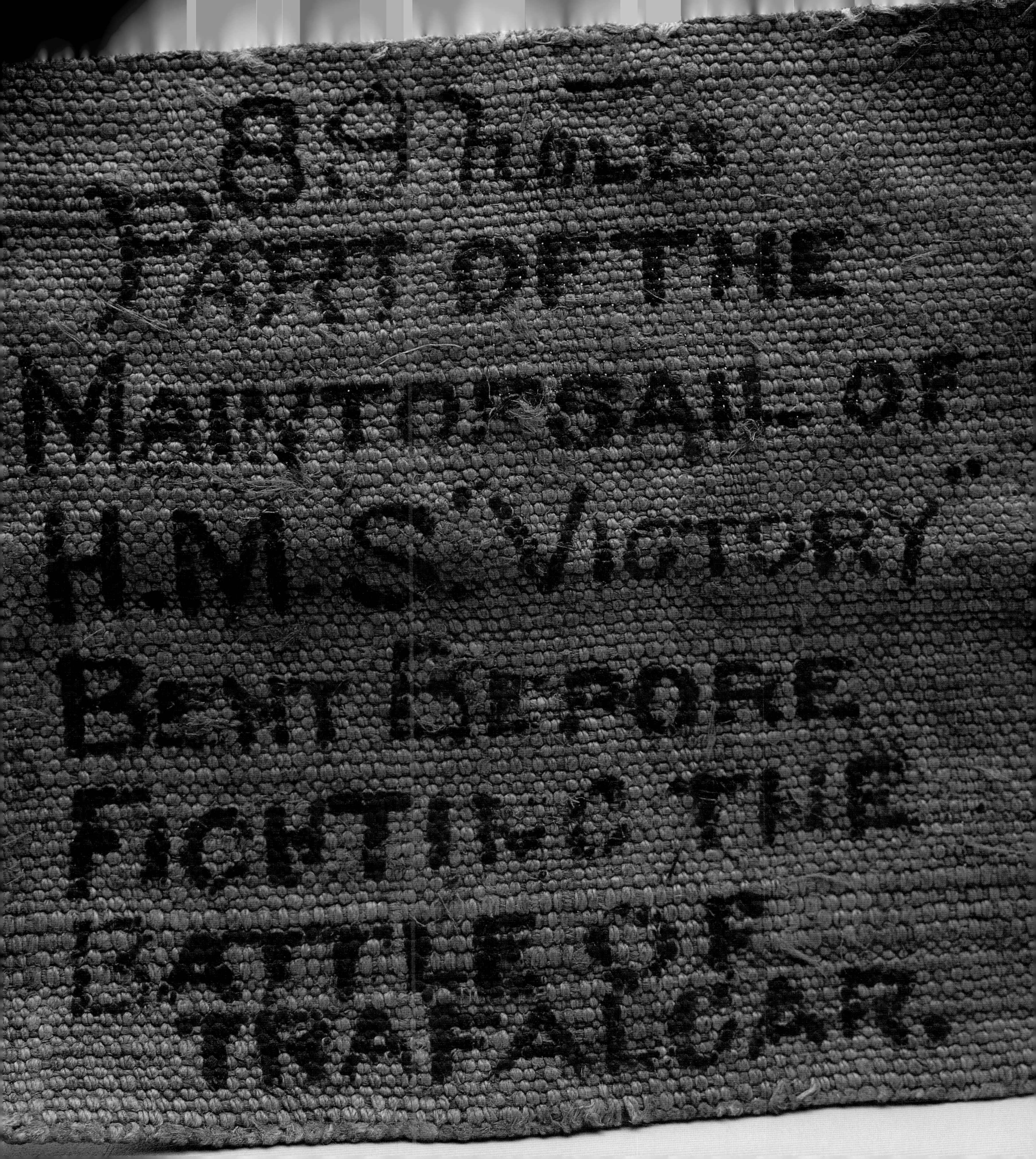

PART OF THE
MAINTOPSAIL OF
H.M.S. VICTORY
BENT BEFORE
FIGHTING THE
BATTLE OF
TRAFALGAR.

PRINT, *"Nelson's First Footing in the Navy"*
Thomas Davidson, painter; from author's collection

This engraving is made after an oil painting by Thomas Davidson, *"Nelson's First Footing in the Navy, Chatham."* The painter is known to have worked in the later half of the nineteenth century, nearly a hundred years from the actual event. The artist is also known for rendering costume and deck layout with a high degree of accuracy.

Nelson's family used the influence of a maternal uncle, Captain Maurice Suckling, to secure young Horatio a slot as "ship's boy" on the HMS *Raisonnable* in the year 1771, when Nelson was twelve years old.

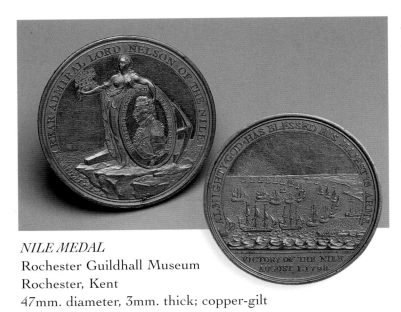

NILE MEDAL
Rochester Guildhall Museum
Rochester, Kent
47mm. diameter, 3mm. thick; copper-gilt

This medal was issued to all members of the English fleet following Nelson's victory at the Battle of the Nile, August 1, 1798. The medals were struck at the expense of Alexander Davison, Nelson's prize agent, with the approval of King George III. Seamen and marines were given copper; petty officers received copper-gilt (example above); lieutenants and warrant officers, sterling silver. Nelson and his captains were presented with gold.

On the front side (above left), the central figure is holding an olive branch and standing in front of an anchor. "Rear-Admiral Lord Nelson of The Nile" is written along the edge. The figure holds an oval with Nelson's profile surrounded by the words "Europe's Hope and Britain's Glory."

The reverse side was meant literally to depict the lines of battle, though it contains a glaring error. In his haste, the engraver has rendered the scene in mirror image, reversing the seascape, ship's course and sun's position in the sky.

NELSON'S MEMORIAL BANNER
Madron Parish Church, Penzance, Cornwall
1m. square; painted fabric on a wooden frame

The Madron Parish Church provides the history of this banner: "The news of the victory at Trafalgar in 1805, and the death of Admiral Nelson, was first brought to England by a Penzance fishing boat, which received the news from HMS *Pickle*, returning from the battle. The fishermen informed the Mayor. A memorial service for Nelson, and a Thanksgiving for the victory of Trafalgar was arranged; the banner was hastily made, and carried before the Mayor and Burgesses in procession to Madron, at that time the Parish Church of Penzance. For many years now a Trafalgar Service has been an annual event at Madron on the Sunday nearest to October twenty-first. The Royal Navy send one of their Ships into port, and naval personnel and members of other maritime services come to the Service. The old banner is put on a pole for the occasion, and carried in procession."

Nelson made it known that he did not wish to be buried at sea. Upon his death, Dr. William Beatty, the ship's surgeon who had attended him, performed an autopsy and removed the musket ball that had pierced his lung and lodged against his spine. His body was placed in a 159-gallon cask filled with brandy and topped off with "spirits of wine." A dispatch boat, the schooner HMS *Pickle*, was selected to speed back to England with the news.

"Mourn for the Brave the immortal Nelson's gone.
His last sea fight is fought his work of Glory done."

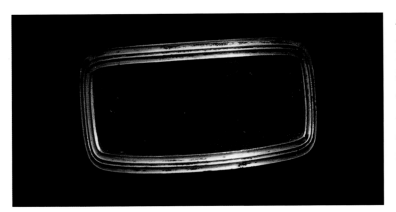

NELSON'S SHOE BUCKLE
Morris Maritime Museum, Penzance, Cornwall
Leather and gilded brass
7cm. wide

This is a simple and understated personal effect from a man who was known for flamboyant dress. At the peak of his celebrity, he embellished his daily costume with jewels, feathers, medallions, insignias, furs and the like.

CERAMIC COMMEMORATIVE URN
Rochester Guildhall Museum, Rochester, Kent
155mm. wide, 120mm. high

This urn commemorates Lord Nelson's heroic death at the Battle of Trafalgar. Thousands of such keepsakes were collected by a grateful nation. The urn is a black vitreous stoneware called basalt ware. It had no maker's mark of any kind, but the museum curators believe that it was made at Wedgewood's Etruria Works at Staffordshire.

The Angelic figure on the side of the urn writes: "Pro Patria [For Country] Nelson, Oct. 21." A second figure looks on. The classic Greek key motif decorates the side as well as the lid handle.

TRAFALGAR BOX
Hartlepool Historic Quay Museum
Hartlepool, Teesside
11cm. wide

This wooden box was made from the timbers of HMS *Victory*. The edges were carved with Nelson's famous signal: "England Expects That Every Man Will Do His Duty," along with an anchor and ropework on the lid.

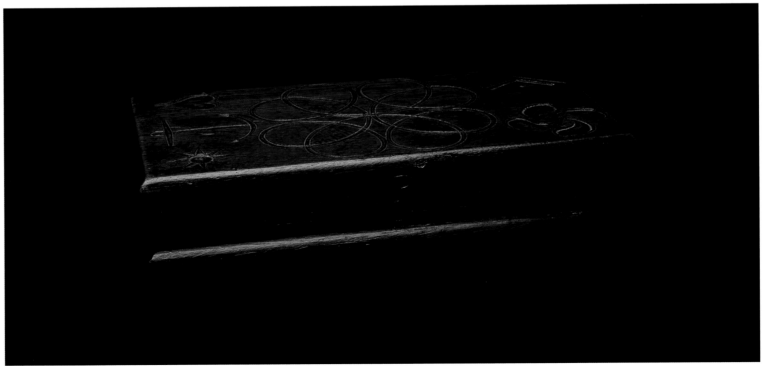

NELSON'S WINE LETTER

Plymouth Naval Base Museum, Plymouth, Devon
30cm. long

This bill of sale for the purchase of a large quantity of marsala wine was obviously drawn up by the merchant John Woodhouse in March of 1800. Nelson's own handwritten comments are followed by his signature. Nelson's penmanship may reflect the fact that he lost his right arm to a musketball about two and a half years earlier at Santa Cruz, Tenerife, in the Canary Islands. The contract assumes that the wine will be poured into existing containers on the ships.

"An agreement made and entered into by the Right Honorable Rear Admiral Horatio Lord Nelson K.B. [Knight of Bath] Duke of Bronte in Sicily &c. &c. with John and William Woodhouse Merchants of Marsala at Palermo the 19th day of March 1800 to furnish His Majesty's Ships off Malta with five hundred pipes of the best Marsala Wine to be delivered there free of freight and all other charges without loss of time at One Shilling and five pence Sterling per Gallon Wine measure and to be paid for in Bills upon the Commissioners for Victualing His Majesty's Navy at the usual date by the respective Pursers of His Majesty's Ships to which the wine is delivered and should any of the casks be wanted with the wine an additional Charge is to be added of One pound Sterling each pipe."

Webster's Complete Dictionary of England defines "pipe" as follows: "A large wine cask of varying capacity; such a cask with its contents; such a cask as a measure of capacity for wine, equal to four barrels, two hogs-heads, or half a tun, and containing 126 wine gallons." At 126 gallons per pipe, this contract for 500 pipes would be 63 thousand gallons.

Continuing in Nelson's hand:
"The wine to be delivered as expeditiously as possible and all to be delivered within the space of five weeks from this date, a convoy will be wanted for the vessel from Marsala but all risks are to be run by Mr. Woodhouse.

Bronte Nelson
For brother & self
John Woodhouse"

Nelson signs his name Bronte Nelson to reflect the fact that he was granted the title Duke of Bronte.

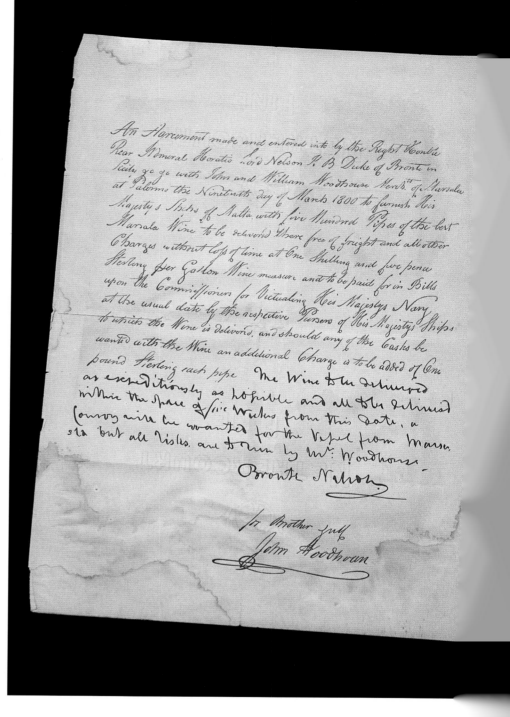

Tar

STOCKHOLM TAR BOX
Morris Maritime Museum, Penzance, Cornwall
1m. wide

"Marline" is a light, two-stranded line that is shown here looped back and forth between the two ends of a wooden box as it is bathed in tar. A crank at one end is turned, which tightens the cord in a "twisting" effect, soaking the fibers and squeezing out the excess. The line can be removed, dried and coiled for future use, or used hot and wet for seizings and other protective wrappings on the ship's standing rigging.

The thick, sticky, black tar was so universally used that the very name became synonymous with the British sailor. A "tar," "Jack Tar" or "Jolly Jack Tar," as he might be called, employed a variety of materials and formulations that came under the name tar. Some versions are a brittle solid at normal temperatures which liquefy when heated. Other formulations remain pliable when cool. There are eighteenth century references to the pitch lakes of Trinidad, pine tar, coal tar, Stockholm tar and bitumen, all of which have found their uses around the ship. Pitch, as in "pitch black," also came under the general category of tar.

Tar was used as a sealant, a preservative and a waterproofing for canvas (tarpaulin). It is said that the way a sailor salutes today, with his palm angled inward, was originally to hide the fact that his hands were likely soiled with tar. Sailors would tar their hats and coats to waterproof them. They would even braid tar into their hair to discourage fleas and lice. Surgeons after amputations would seal off the wound with hot pitch to stop the bleeding and prevent infection.

The planks of the deck and hull were caulked with oakum, old rope fibers impregnated with tar. Records at the Devonport Dockyard in Plymouth indicate that tarring at their ropery in the eighteenth century was carried out by passing the fibers through a hot mixture of tallow (animal fat) and whale oil. Admiralty regulations stated that the quantity of tar put into government ropes must be equal to one-fifth the weight of the white yarns or one-sixth of them when tarred.

Stockholm tar is frequently listed among dockyard supplies, and quantities were carried as part of the ship's stores. It was a generic term for the products of the pine tree and came from Scandinavia, the Baltic countries, Russia and North America.

nd began to hail her friends for that

does thee know a mon neamed Adam

was shaken in sign of ignorance.

hee?

portunities of making acquaintance
limited, and she could not resolve the

man with a wooden leg), Cowskin,
Cock-eye, Pig-tail, and Yellow-belly,
voked, but in vain, and the querist fell
udy, in which she remained for some
wever, her eyes suddenly bright-
of her companions on the
mphantly, "Dash my wig
!" and then turning to
Yo should'n ax'd** for

y frequently, groups of
be seen wandering about
am, with much the same sensa-
experience at New York or Phil-
was at Birmingham that the Roscio-ma-
Byron calls it, first broke out, and in a few
ct rumours of Young Betty's fame caught
en in the coal-mines.   One man, more
ore idle than his fellows, determined to
k, and see the prodigy with his own eyes;
o resolved, he proceeded, although in the
week, to put on a clean shirt and a clean
uld even have anticipated the Saturday
he was preserved from such extravagan
e which prevented Mrs. Gilpin from allow
se to draw up to her door on the eventfu
the journey,

"_____ lest all

Should say that she was proud."

hstanding this moderation he did not pas
The unwonted hue of the shirt and fa
ats not to be disregarded; and he had n
en the road to Birmingham, than he was me
nished brother, whose amazement, when
d vent in words, produced the following d
i say, sirree, where be'st thee gwain'?—
wain to Brummajum."—"What be'st agan
"Oi'm agwain to see the Young Roc
?"—"Oi tell thee Oi'm agwain to see t
ocus."—"Is it aloive?"

You should have asked.

‡ Going.

(Wa?f?shire Colliers.)

The Office of the Society for the Diffusion of Useful Knowledge
38, Lincoln's Inn Fields.
LONDON:—CHARLES KNIGHT, 22, LUDGATE STREET.
Printed by William Clowes and Sons, Stamford Street.

THE PENNY MAGAZINE

OF THE

Society for the Diffusion of Useful Knowledge.

247.]   PUBLISHED EVERY SATURDAY.   [FEBRUARY 6, 1836.

TAR-MAKING IN BOTHNIA.

[Tar-Making.]

TAR is a thick, black gum, obtained from the fir-tree by burning.   Pitch is the name applied to the same article when thickened by boiling.   The vast forests of the north of Europe are necessarily the spots to which the manufacture of tar on an extensive scale is confined.   Thus, in the year 1833, there were imported into Great Britain 10,152 lasts of tar, all of which, with the exception of 1231 lasts, came from the forests of northern Europe.   Russia supplied us with 7980 lasts, Sweden 442, Denmark 415, and Norway 83.   The duty amounted to 7601l.   Each last contains twelve barrels; and a barrel holds about thirty gallons.   The German name for tar is "theer," and the Swedish "tjära," so that the English word is clearly to be traced to a northern origin.

The process of making tar was known to the Greeks, and has been described by Theophrastes and Dioscorides. Dr. Clarke, who has described the method of extracting tar in Russia, Sweden, and other northern countries, says, "There is not the smallest difference between a tar-work in the forests of Westro-Bothnia and those of Ancient Greece.   The Greeks made stacks of pine, and having covered them with turf, they were suffered to

VOL. V.

burn in the same smothered manner; while the tar, melting, fell to the bottom of the stack, and ran out by a small channel cut for the purpose."

The following is Dr. Clarke's account of tar-making in the north of Europe:—"The inlets of the Gulf of Bothnia are surrounded by noble forests, whose tall trees, flourishing luxuriantly, covered the soil quite down to the water's edge.   From the most southern parts of Westro-Bothnia to the northern extremity of the Gulf, the inhabitants are occupied in the manufacture of tar, proofs of which are visible in the whole extent of the coast.   The process by which the tar is obtained is very simple; and as we often witnessed it, we shall now describe it, from a tar-work we halted to inspect upon the spot.   The situation most favourable to the process is in a forest near to a marsh or bog, because the roots of the fir, from which tar is principally extracted, are always most productive in such places.   A conical cavity is then made in the ground (generally in the side of a bank or sloping hill); and the roots of the fir, together with logs and billets of the same, being neatly trussed in a stack of the same conical shape, are let into this cavity.   The whole is

H

FROM THE "PENNY MAGAZINE"
of the "Society for the Diffusion of Useful Knowledge"
February 6, 1836. A weekly publication.
From the library of Mr. William Scott, Proprietor
The Lady Hamilton Inn, The Hard, Portsmouth, Hampshire

The Penny Magazine article at left gives a rare and precise description of the manufacture of tar. The article concludes on a subsequent page: "...then covered with turf, to prevent the volatile parts from being dissipated, which by means of a heavy wooden mallet, and a wooden stamper worked separately by two men, is beaten down and rendered as firm as possible above the wood. The stack of billets is then kindled, and a slow combustion of the fir takes place, without flame, as in making charcoal. During this combustion the tar exudes; and a cast-iron pan being at the bottom of the funnel, with a spout which projects through the side of the bank, barrels are placed beneath this spout to collect the fluid as it comes away. As fast as the barrels are filled, they are bunged and made ready for exportation. From this description it will be evident that the mode of obtaining tar is by a kind of distillation per descensum; the turpentine, melted by the fire, mixing with the sap and juices of the fir, while the wood itself, becoming charred, is converted into charcoal."

HOT TAR LADLE, two views
Morris Maritime Museum, Penzance, Cornwall
65cm. long

This beautifully designed tool is meant to pour a controlled drip of hot tar into the seams between the deck planks.

Many captains were sticklers for keeping the planks spotless. The upper decks in warm weather would be splattered with drips of tar that fell from the strands of rope in the rigging. Daily scrubbing with large abrasive holystones, so called because they resembled bibles, kept the decks snowy white. The ropes themselves would also shed fibers that accumulated on the decks. This "shake" was swept up and used for oakum.

Sailors have an expression for a formidable task for which they are ill prepared: "We've got the devil to pay and no pitch hot." Filling a seam with oakum and tar was called "paying" the seam. The "devil" was the last, outboard plank on the deck; it was difficult to get at and required a lot of filler.

Similarly, when a sailor went overboard he was "between the devil and the deep blue sea."

ORIGINAL GUN DECK of HMS Victory
Portsmouth, Hampshire

When a wooden warship of the eighteenth century was launched, a thirty-year useful life was about all that could be expected. Those few ships that have managed to survive the 150 or 200 years to the present day have done so by being periodically renewed, rebuilt and refitted to a point where one might ask if any timbers survive from the original launch.

HMS *Victory* was a forty-year-old ship in 1805 when she fought at Trafalgar and had already undergone extensive refittings in 1780 and 1801. The hammering she endured in Nelson's final battle would put her in the repair yard at Chatham for a considerable time, and there was discussion as to whether she could ever be returned to fighting trim. With all the effort that has gone into her conservation, the gun deck, pictured above, survives battle scarred but still sound.

DECK REPAIR from HMS Warrior
Portsmouth, Hampshire

The ship dates from a later era (launched in 1860), but the rot caused by water seeping in between the cracks was common to all ships.

A narrow channel has been rabbeted along the length of both replacement planks as well as across the ends. Oakum would be forced down into the crack where the two surfaces meet, and the channel filled with hot pitch. The recessed hole for the spike would be similarly caulked, then plugged with a wooden peg that was cut off flush with the deck.

UPPER DECK from HMS Victory
Portsmouth, Hampshire

Daily scrubbing of the decks was sometimes seen as a make-work discipline. The upper decks were open and exposed to the hot sun and would benefit from a daily swab to keep from drying and shrinking. The enclosed, lower decks where men ate and slept were also scrubbed each morning, often using vinegar as a disinfectant. There are instances where the ship's surgeon petitioned the captain to discontinue the daily washing of the lower decks because it created damp conditions that caused the men to suffer from rheumatism and other health problems.

BESOM BROOM and HANDLE
Chatham Historic
Dockyard, Chatham, Kent
120cm. long

Many of these brooms were found aboard HMS *Invincible*. They were used for cleaning the underwater portion of the ship's hull in a process known as breaming. The operation could be carried out in a repair dock or in shallow water where the low tide exposes the hull.

Falconer's Dictionary of the Marine, published in 1769, describes the process as follows: "To bream: To burn off the filth such as grass, ooze, shells or seaweed from the ship's-bottom that has gathered to it in a voyage or by lying long in a harbor. This operation is performed by holding a kindled furze, faggots or such material to the bottom so that the flame incorporating with the pitch, sulphur etc. that had formerly covered it immediately loosens and throws off whatever filth may have adhered to the planks."

TAR BRUSH from HMS Invincible
Chatham Historic Dockyard, Chatham, Kent
35cm. long

A modern brush would have a metal ferrule to hold the bristles in place. Here, the animal hairs are bound to the wooden handle with cotton twine.

Navigation

OCTANT

Hartlepool Historic Quay, Hartlepool, Teesside

35cm. tall

This elegant navigation instrument rests on top of its wooden case. The eyepiece rests to the left. It was made by William Mowbray of West Hartlepool. It's called an "octant" because its scale represents an eighth of a circle.

From midshipmen up through the junior officers, everyone was expected to own the instruments that were basic to the navigation of the ship. Midshipmen were schooled daily in the science of navigation. By measuring the angle of a known celestial body and the horizon, and recording the exact time of the sighting and then consulting a book of tables, it was possible to determine an inexact but useful indication of the ship's position at sea.

SHIP'S TELESCOPE
Hartlepool Historic Quay Museum, Hartlepool, Teesside
43cm. long

The precisely ground glass lenses are mounted in these brass tubes with glazed cloth covering, bound with twine. There is a sliding shutter at one end to function as a lens cap. Maximum telescopic power is achieved by pulling or "drawing" out all the concentric tubes to the instrument's full length. This telescope when fully extended is 118cm. Because of the two additional tubes nested in the body, it is referred to as a "two draw," or sometimes "two drawer."

On a clear day at sea a ship's view to the horizon in all directions adds up to well over 1500 square miles. Spotting the upper parts of a ship that is still "hull down" over the horizon increases the field considerably. In time of war, information about

the presence of another ship, friend or foe, is valuable intelligence. A sharp lookout with a telescope could receive signals, discern distant landmarks, and determine another vessel's course, rig, nationality and intentions.

In low light situations at dusk, dawn, the dead of night, or in foul weather, ships were equipped with a "night glass," a telescope that provided a brighter view, with the slight inconvenience of the image being upside down.

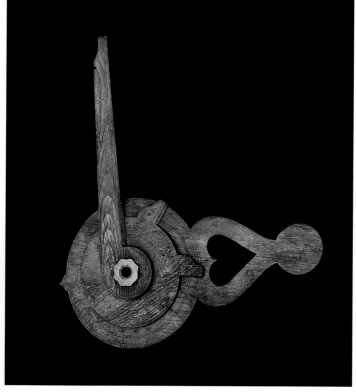

NOCTURNAL
Morris Maritime Museum, Penzance, Cornwall
20cm. from top to bottom

The "nocturnal" was a wooden instrument used aboard ship to determine time at night. The concentric circular scales could be rotated independently. In English waters the device was calibrated for the "pointer stars of the Great Bear," Ursa Major.

A sailor would view the pole star through the center hole. If he has accurately dialed in the correct month, day and position of each of the pointer stars, he is able to read a separate scale to determine the time interval before or after midnight.

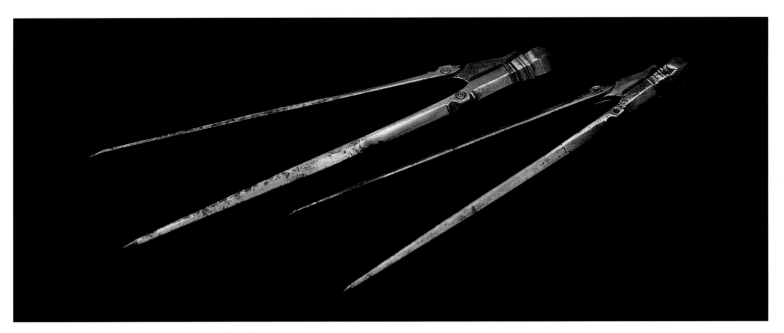

DIVIDERS
Morris Maritime Museum, Penzance, Cornwall
17cm. long

By spreading the points of the divider to the scale at the edge of a nautical chart, the navigator can then "walk off" the distance between two locations.

SHIP'S LEAD
Falmouth Maritime Museum
Falmouth, Cornwall
31cm. long

The captain of the ship needs constant assurance that there is a safe depth beneath his hull. A weighted line with a system of knots or marks could be read to determine depth "soundings." The ship's lead (pronounced "led") was normally attached to a line twenty fathoms (120ft.) long.

The leadsman stood in the "chains" at the ship's side and hurled the lead forward so that as it sank it was near vertical as it struck bottom. The underside of the lead had a spoon-shaped hollow that could be "armed" with sticky tallow or grease to retrieve a sample of the sea bottom and identify sand, rock, mud, shells, grass or gravel.

The lead weighed approximately seven pounds. The deep-water line was up to 200 fathoms (1200ft.) long, with a lead of fourteen to thirty pounds.

SAND GLASSES
Chatham Historic Dockyard Museum, Chatham, Kent
127mm., 150mm. overall height

Sand Glasses recovered from HMS *Invincible*. They were used to keep time on board ship. The larger half-hour glass was used to time the ringing of the ship's bell to ensure that the watch, the lookouts and sentries were properly relieved. The four-hour watch was split into eight thirty-minute "tricks"; at the turn of each trick the helmsman was relieved and a bell sounded.

The smaller glass of twenty-eight seconds was used to time the log line as it ran out measuring the ship's speed through the water. Sand glasses of fourteen seconds' duration have also been found aboard HMS *Invincible*, indicating that she was considered a very fast ship. Both glasses have oak ends decorated with concentric circles and marked with a broad arrow. The struts are pine, the packing is beech.

The upper and lower sand chambers are two distinct, pear-shaped blown glass vessels with an opening at each tapered end. The two halves are fitted tightly together separated only by a small copper wafer with a precisely drilled hole through its center. This "regulator disk" assures a consistent measurement of the time it takes all the sand to fall to the lower chamber. The whole "waist" area was sealed with pitch or wax and wrapped with twine to insure that the sand did not become damp.

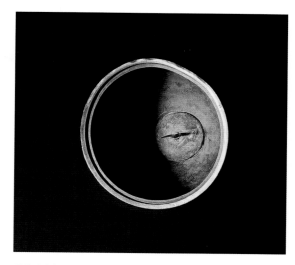

BRASS BOWL
Chatham Historic Dockyard Museum
Chatham, Kent
12.5cm. across

This deep brass bowl with a slender spike projecting up from the bottom would have had the "compass card" balanced on the point, floating in alcohol or spirits and sealed under a clear glass top. The "card" is actually a round disc of very light wood or treated paper with the compass needle embedded inside. Even when the ship was heeled over at an angle, the markings on the card would show the heading. It was recovered from HMS *Invincible*.

Food and Drink

PEWTER PLATE, BOWL and SPOON from HMS Invincible
Chatham Historic Dockyard Museum, Chatham, Kent

This metal dinnerware is battered and distressed after more than 200 years at the bottom of the sea. In use aboard HMS *Invincible*, it would have been kept brightly polished for use by the officers. This service was starkly contrasted with the crude utensils used by the common sailors.

ROUND BISCUIT
Plymouth Naval Base Museum
Plymouth, Devon
12cm. across

In port, the men were usually supplied with fresh bread, but at sea they would be served a hard but wholesome "ship's biscuit." These would have been baked at one of several victualling yards and carefully sealed in barrels for use on extended cruises.

SIX-SIDED SHIP'S BISCUIT
Plymouth Naval Base Museum
Plymouth, Devon
15cm. across

The shape could vary, but the specifications required that the weight of each be such that there were "not less than five to the pound." The ship was to be provisioned to ensure a daily ration of "one pound of bread per day" for each man. This biscuit is marked with the broad arrow, and a "D," which indicates the victualling yard at Devonport, Plymouth.

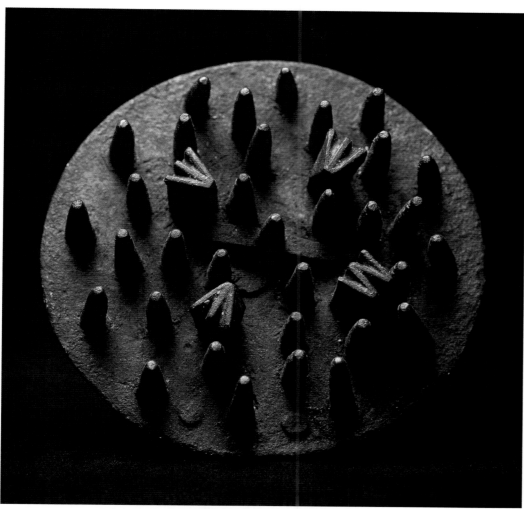

IRON BISCUIT PRESS
Plymouth Naval Base Museum
Plymouth, Devon
12cm. across

When the baker's hand press dimples the dough before baking, it is marking it (three times) with the broad arrow, and also identifying which victualling yard it came from, in this case, a "W," for Woolwich.

IRON BISCUIT PRESS
Plymouth Naval Base Museum
Plymouth, Devon
12cm. across

The back side of the baker's biscuit press (above) shows that each little iron "finger" was individually forged into the tool, and the arrows and "W" are held in place by pins. A crack on the near edge has been neatly repaired by the smith. The handle is wooden.

TURNED WOODEN BOWL from HMS Invincible
Chatham Historic Dockyard Museum, Chatham, Kent
Elm; 30cm. diameter, wall thickness 18mm.

Turned wooden bowl from HMS *Invincible*. Empty or full, there is no doubt that this is government property. The broad arrow is deeply scored into the bottom of the bowl and repeated eight times around the rim.

TURNED WOODEN BOWL from HMS Invincible, *underside view*
Chatham Historic Dockyard Museum, Chatham, Kent

The sailors have added to the two broad arrows on the bottom of the bowl
with their own mark: a hangman's gallows.

WOODEN BUNG for Sealing a Barrel
Chatham Historic Dockyard Museum, Chatham, Kent
8cm. in diameter

A great many of the ship's provisions and stores, both wet and dry, were stored in barrels. To create space as supplies were consumed, the coopers would carefully disassemble the barrels and store the parts for later reuse.

There was the inevitable breakage, not to mention attack from rats, that caused all manner of liquids to seep down into the ballast stones and bilges, making the hold a foul and unhealthy place.

BRONZE SPIRIT TAP from HMS Invincible
Chatham Historic Dockyard Museum, Chatham, Kent
11.5cm. across

The handle at the top, which has broken off, was originally heart shaped.

Beer and sometimes wine were readily available aboard ship, and was in fact preferred to water, which never tasted fresh. Spirits, on the other hand, were meted out carefully. The men's rum tot was rationed in such a way as to prevent rowdy drunkenness and inability to work the ship. Stronger drink was certainly aboard as the personal property of the officers, but forbidden to ordinary sailors. Rum, gin, whisky, brandy and the like were stored in the "spirits locker," which on some vessels was a sizable room guarded night and day by an armed marine.

RUM BARREL from HMS Invincible
Chatham Historic Dockyard
Museum, Chatham, Kent
45cm. high

The sailor's legendary daily ration of rum was by no means a universal privilege. It varied according to the ship, the season, the locale, and other factors. The tot was generally figured at one half-pint per man per day. It was often mixed with two parts' water and meted out half at noon and half in the evening to prevent hoarding and bingeing.

Lime juice was often added to the mixture, not in the interest of making a tasty cocktail but rather to prevent scurvy.

WOODEN BARREL TAP from HMS Invincible
Chatham Historic Dockyard Museum, Chatham, Kent
13cm. long

By removing the bung or plug that sealed the barrel, this tap could be inserted into the hole to pour out the contents. In cases where the fluids were more precious, as in an officer's brandy or whisky supply, he might have a more elaborate metal tap that would conserve every drop. Some of these spirit taps required a separate key to dispense the liquor.

TANKARD, Recovered from HMS Invincible
Chatham Historic Dockyard Museum, Chatham, Kent
16.6cm. tall

The base, handle and lid are oak. The sides are built up of individual wooden staves, like a barrel. These staves are made up of lignum vitae, "the wood of life," a dense, water-resistant hardwood. The bottom is wider for stability on a tossing ship. The lid is delicately carved with the figure of an oak tree, a reminder of home perhaps.

CONE-SHAPED BASKET
Chatham Historic Dockyard Museum, Chatham, Kent
50cm. long

The exact purpose of this simple basket is not known. It was recovered from HMS *Invincible*. Various uses have been suggested, based upon drawings and illustrations of the period. It could have been used as a collander, strainer or sieve in food preparation, or for gathering mollusks or small fish. Its construction of wooden splints woven around stout twigs was similarly used in making eel and fish traps.

SAILOR'S WOODEN DRINKING MUG
Royal Marines Museum, Portsea, Hampshire
15cm. tall

Coopers were very skilled hands on a British warship. Gunpowder, water, wine, preserved meats, biscuits, and a host of other provisions required a sturdy, tightly sealed barrel. The same techniques would be used for personal items that please the eye and function nicely.

PEWTER TANKARD
Padstow Shipwreck Museum, Padstow, Cornwall
18cm. tall

Fresh water was a precious commodity aboard ship. A man-of-war with a crew numbering in excess of 500 men would set out for an extended cruise with nearly thirty tons of water stored below deck in huge wooden casks. In spite of every attempt to keep the supply from becoming contaminated, it would often become cloudy, foul smelling and rank.

Beer, ale, cider and wine, however, kept quite well, and vast stores were provided for the men. Victualling records show that the potency of that beer was kept quite mild and, was made available in unlimited supply. It is said that some men drank no water at all when at sea. Ships would often anchor in the shallow water off the town of Deal in southeast England to replenish their supply of fresh water and beer. If the men had recently fought bravely or if morale needed a boost, the requisition might specify a quantity of "strong beer."

STONEWARE JUG
from HMS Invincible
Chatham Historic Dockyard
Museum,Chatham, Kent
24cm. tall

This stoneware jug with lipped neck and broken handle was examined by scientists at Portsmouth Polytechnic and found to have contained animal fats, possibly for cooking.

SHERRY and MADIERA BOTTLES from HMS Invincible
Chatham Historic Dockyard Museum, Chatham, Kent
23cm. tall (left), 25cm (right)

Great quantities of wine were drunk aboard ship. Most of it would be drawn from large casks among the purser's stores. This sherry bottle at left and the Madeira bottle opposite were probably of better quality and the personal property of one of the officers.

WOODEN BUCKET from HMS Invincible
Chatham Historic Dockyard Museum
38cm. wide, 25cm. tall

A stave-built oak save-all or bucket, with wicker binding and pegged oak bottom. Scored with a broad arrow.

This half-barrel bucket would have been shared by mess mates. It was used to carry provisions from the galley or to clean the decks. During battle, it could be filled with seawater for damp sponging the cannon bores between shots.

When recovered from HMS *Invincible*, the rope handle was intact.

SQUARE OAK PLATE
Chatham Historic Dockyard
Museum, Chatham, Kent
30cm. square

Rather than the pewter or china service used by the officers, this humble oak plate with raised sides is what the sailors used. It's thought to be the inspiration for the term "three square meals a day."

The raised side, which keeps the food from dripping or sliding away, is called a "fiddle."

WOODEN TALLEY STICK
from HMS Invicible
Chatham Historic Dockyard Museum, Chatham, Kent
13.5cm.

A "tally stick" is the eighteenth century version of a modern "tie-on" label and had many uses, from labeling sails and stores to identifying a sailor's personal property.

Rope

CABLE LAID ROPE
Padstow Shipwreck Museum, Padstow, Cornwall
23cm. in circumference

The ropery at Chatham in the mid-1790s began by drying and untangling hemp fibers, which were then combed into "yarns." The yarns were spun into "threads" and the threads were twisted into "strands". The strands could be combined or "closed" in various ways.

The usual three-strand rope is said to be "hawser laid." When two strands of two are combined, for a total of four strands, it becomes "shroud laid." When three hawser laid ropes are twisted together into nine strands, the rope is said to be "cable laid."

When a ship "slips its cable" it leaves in a hurry, sometimes in stealth, sometimes in danger. It doesn't bother to retrieve the anchor, it just cuts the rope or throws the bitter end over the side and sails away. When a sailor has "slipped his cable" he has died or "gone to Davy Jones Locker."

SERVING MALLET
Recovered from HMS *Invincible*
Chatham Historic Dockyard Museum, Chatham, Kent
30.5cm. long

Serving protects a rope from chafing and other wear by wrapping a smaller rope or twine around it. The groove in the head of this tool is laid against the length of rope to be served, and the smaller rope is twined around the head and handle in such a way that gives leverage and provides tension for a tight wrap.

SERVED and SEIZED ROPE
Recovered from HMS *Invincible*
Chatham Historic Dockyard Museum, Chatham, Kent
23cm. in circumference

The underlying rope, which is nine inches (229mm.) in circumference, has been tightly wrapped (served) with a coil of smaller rope. Two pieces of the served rope have been laid side by side and lashed together (seized). The rope was then coated with tar. The fact that it survived 220 years at the bottom of the sea shows the properties of tar. The rope was probably part of HMS *Invincible*'s shrouds or stays, the "standing rigging" that supported the masts.

THE ADMIRAL'S FID
HMS *Warrior*, HM Naval Base, Portsmouth, Hampshire
80cm. long

Fids are pins used for opening strands of rope for splicing, sewing and making grommets. This is a much larger version of the metal marline spike that all seamen carried with them. It was jokingly called the admiral's fid because of its great size.

Resembling a very fat baseball bat, it was used to hold open the huge strands of the ship's anchor cable and other large ropes when splicing.

SERVING MALLET
HMS *Warrior*, HM Naval Base, Portsmouth, Hampshire
25cm. long

This is a contemporary serving mallet in use aboard HMS *Warrior*. The grooves worn into it trace the path of the twine that is wrapped around a larger rope to protect it and increase its life.

ROPEWALK
Devonport Royal Navy Dockyard, Plymouth, Devon

The Devonport Royal Navy Dockyard in Plymouth was one of three principal sites that "closed rope" for the ships of the Royal Navy. The ropery operation consisted of cleaning and combing, or "hatchelling," the raw fibers, spinning the fibers into yarn and then laying the yarns out to be twisted into strands. When completed strands are twisted together to give the rope its final shape it is referred to as "closed."

Before the advent of spinning machinery, a ropemaker or spinner walked backwards down the full length of the rope-house with a bundle of hemp wrapped around his waist weighing 29.5 kilograms. This "laying floor" in Plymouth was designed to be fireproof. The walls are stone and the supporting columns and ceiling panels are cast iron. The roof is of slate and clay tiles.

The standard length for rope supplied for navy use was 120 fathoms (720ft). This figure was based upon the idea that a ship-of-the-line would not anchor in water more than forty fathoms deep. By allowing up to three times the depth of the water, it gave the ship a more horizontal pull against the anchor, and thus a better purchase on the seabed.

The building had to be very long, because as the rope was twisted it got shorter. Some ropeyard buildings were one-quarter of a mile long.

MIZZEN MAST
HMS *Victory*, HM Naval Base, Portsmouth, Hampshire
It rises 48.8 meters above the waterline.

This is the view looking up the mizzen mast on HMS *Victory*. A first-rate ship-of-the-line such as HMS *Victory* required about thirty miles of rope, which, along with the reserve cordage that the ship carried, would weigh in the area of forty-eight tons.

A young midshipman, writing home to his family after the battle at Trafalgar, reported that *Victory's* mizzen mast had been shot away about nine feet above deck.

Deckgear and Rigging

BELAYING PIN and RACK
Chatham Historic Dockyard Museum, Chatham, Kent
120cm. long

Racks of belaying pins were mounted at various places around the upper deck to secure the ropes of the running rigging. The sailor would "make the line fast" by looping it repeatedly in a figure-8 fashion, first under the lower extension of the racked pin and then up around the "handle." Tension on each line controlling a sail can be increased or eased. This pin and rack were found together on HMS *Invincible*. Belaying pins were typically turned from a single piece of ash or elm.

From *Falconer's Dictionary of the Marine:*
"To belay: to fasten a rope by winding it several times around a cleat, belaying pin or kevel. This term is peculiar to small ropes and chiefly the running rigging. There being several other expressions used for larger ropes as: bighting, bending, making fast, stoppering."

In theory, the belaying system works as a safety fuse. If a sail or some part of the rigging is suddenly subjected to a dangerous strain such as a severe gust of wind, the figure-8 winding acts to snap the pin in half and free the rope, thus easing the strain, and saving a split sail or a parted line.

MAST POND
Chatham Historic Dockyard, Chatham, Kent

Dockyards would often have acres of shallow mast ponds to store the select timber that would be fashioned into the ship's masts or spars. With the bark left on and floating in salt water, the wood was left for years to season, or pickle. This kept the wood from becoming brittle from the loss of the tree's natural resins. The buoyant storage also insured that the long timbers would remain straight and true.

SNATCH BLOCK
Chatham Historic Dockyard Museum, Chatham, Kent
35cm. long

The shell of the block is nicely carved from a single piece of elm. The sheave (pulley) and axle pin are carved from lignum vitae, which is extremely tough and rot resistant, and constantly exudes a waxy resin, acting to lubricate the moving parts. Note that one side of the shell is open to receive a length of rope. A ship-of-the-line such as HMS *Invincible* required roughly one thousand blocks of varying designs as part of her running rigging.

PART of a PARREL SET
Chatham Historic Dockyard Museum, Chatham, Kent
Rib is 30cm long, truck is 7cm. in diameter

A "parrel set" is a roller that kept the horizontal spar (the "yard") from chafing under the intense friction generated as the sailors raised and lowered this heavy cross member or as the force of the wind caused it to "work" against the vertical mast.

A full parrel assembly would form a collar, much like a beaded necklace, around the mast of up to 16 "trucks" (the spherical walnut rollers), separated by the ash or elm "ribs."

FRIGATE SECTION
Hartlepool Historic Quay Museum, Hartlepool, Teesside
92cm. from base to top of mast

This superbly constructed model was made in mahogany. It neatly shows the mast's supporting "standing rigging." The base shows some sailor's fancy ropework, with turk's head knots for feet and Portuguese-style basketweave, called sente, around the lower mounting base. Models such as this could be the work of the shipyard, which would present them to the VIPs at the admiralty, or simply the work of a skilled sailor with time on his hands.

The frigates were well armed, but smaller and faster than the ships-of-the-line. They were largely used in single ship actions but often performed valuable noncombat roles during fleet action, such as relaying signals. There was a general convention that nearby frigates would not be fired upon during a battle by enemy ships-of-the-line unless the frigate's behavior was deemed to be "provocative."

Admiral Lord Nelson thought frigates so valuable in 1798 that he said: "Was I to die at this moment, *want of frigates* would be found stamped on my heart."

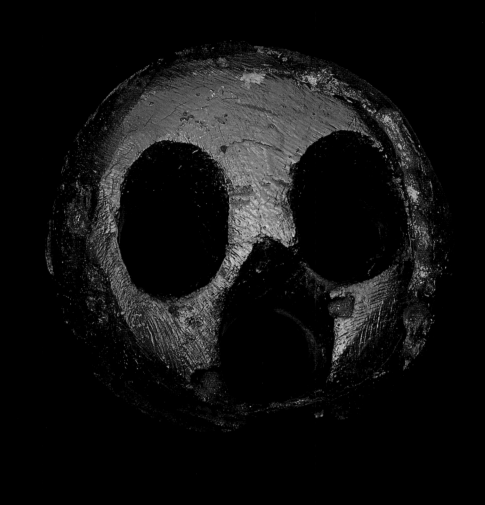

DEADEYE
Morris Maritime Museum, Penzance, Cornwall
22cm. long

A deadeye is so called because the sailors felt it looked like a skull. It has no moving parts and was often carved from a single piece of elm. When mounted in pairs and threaded with a single piece of rope, the rope, or lanyard, can be pulled to tighten and then secure the standing or semi-permanent rigging. Such a rig has the same mechanical advantage as two triple blocks.

DEADEYES on HMS Victory
Portsmouth, Hampshire

Deadeyes are part of HMS *Victory*'s standing rigging, which is more or less permanently adjusted to oppose the pressure that the wind puts on the sails, and thus on the masts, as the ship is driven forward. The shrouds are the tarred ropes that are attached to points high up on the mast, terminating in deadeyes on deck. A second deadeye below is firmly affixed to the "chains," metal fasteners that are bolted into the ship's main structural timbers. The white rope lanyards, threaded through the three holes or eyes in each deadeye, can adjust tension in the shroud above.

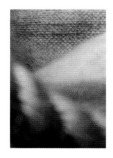

Sails

SAIL

Sail Loft, Chatham Historic Dockyard, Chatham, Kent

HMS *Victory* carried a suit of thirty-six sails that covered nearly four acres (1.6 hectares). Every sail was made up of a number of panels of canvas, just two feet wide. Each sail had to be stitched by hand using a double flat seam with between 108 and 116 stitches to the yard.

The master sailmaker was considered an artisan and had the status of a warrant officer, and as such was exempt from the seaman's menial duties. In civilan life, he could not be pressed into naval service. He worked from narrow bolts of sturdy navy canvas in varying weights to make and repair sails, fashion awnings, hammocks, buckets, boat covers, tarpaulins and dozens of other useful objects. He even made his own work clothes which we would recognize as bib-overalls. His handiwork was tested in gale-force winds and in the heat of sea battles.

Royal Navy canvas was made in various weights to the admiralty's exacting specifications. The warp was flax. The weft was hemp. Bolts were supplied 40 meters (130ft.) long and 600mm. (2ft.) wide. The entire outer edge of each sail was sewn to a bolt rope with twine waxed with a mixture of beeswax and turpentine. This twine was also made with great care. The admiralty's requirements were: "The best English made twine of three threads spun 360 fathoms (2160ft.) to the pound."

At the roperies in the royal dockyards the job of spinning both rope and twine was a highly skilled craft that was often taught to the widows of seamen. At times, the demand for quality twine was such that the spinners were offered triple pay.

Opposite is a sail showing the bolt rope, which is stitched around the entire perimeter, finishing and reinforcing the sail.

SAILMAKER'S FID

Hartlepool Historic Quay Museum, Hartlepool, Teesside
21 and 19cm. long

The fid on the left is hardwood, with a grip made of "marline" woven into a "double diamond" knot. The tool on the right has a wooden handle with a metal spike. The rounded end is designed to fit nicely in the hand.

BONE FID

Hartlepool Historic Quay Museum, Hartlepool, Teesside
14.5cm. long

SNUFFBOX with WARSHIP DESIGN

Hartlepool Historic Quay Museum, Hartlepool, Teesside
5.5cm. wide

This snuffbox was made of papier-mâché. The warship on the cover shows the sail construction, which was built up from two-foot bolts of canvas.

SAILMAKER'S SEAM RUBBERS
Hartlepool Historic Quay Museum, Hartlepool, Teesside
Tool on left is 9cm. long

These were used to flatten the bulky seams that have just been sewn in a sail. These simple tools, each carved from a single piece of wood, show a very sophisticated sense of design and indicate great pride of craftsmanship.

SAILMAKER'S FID
Sailmaker's Loft, Chatham Historic Dockyard,
Chatham, Kent
25cm. long

This simple tool made from a single piece of wood
is worn smooth from years of use.

ROPE SERVING TOOL
Falmouth Maritime Museum, Falmouth, Cornwall
21.5cm. long

Like the serving mallet, this tool was used to wrap
a lighter line in a tight, protective coil around a
regular twisted rope.

SERVING TOOLS
Falmouth Maritime Museum, Falmouth, Cornwall
Foreground tool, 27cm. long; background tool, 21cm. long

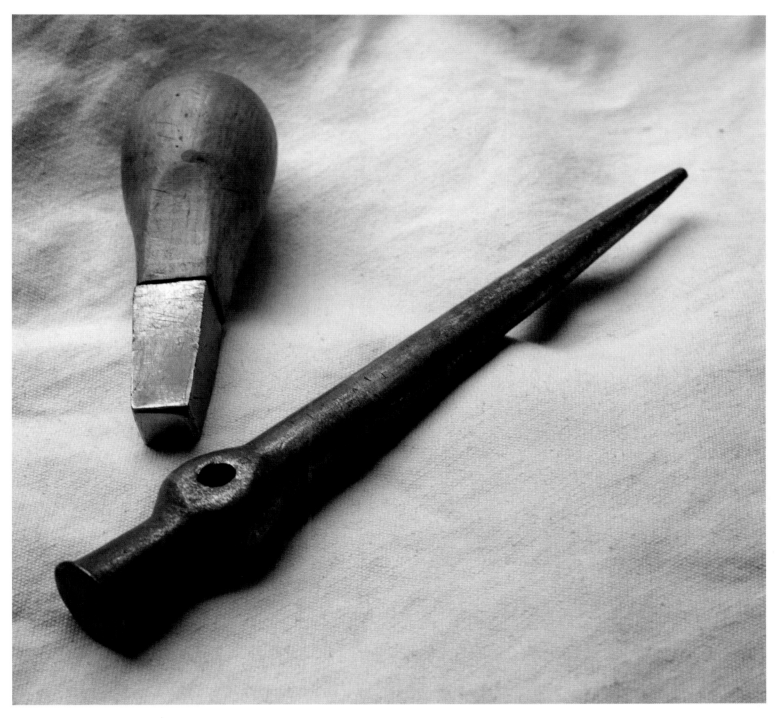

SAILMAKER'S TOOLS
Sailmaker's Loft, Chatham Historic Dockyard, Chatham, Kent
Spike, 19.5cm. long

The metal seam rubber has a wooden handle. The iron fid or "marlinspike" was forged with a hole to allow a loop of cord to be threaded through to form a lanyard for safely carrying the tool aloft. The hole could also be the eye of the needle for fancy ropework.

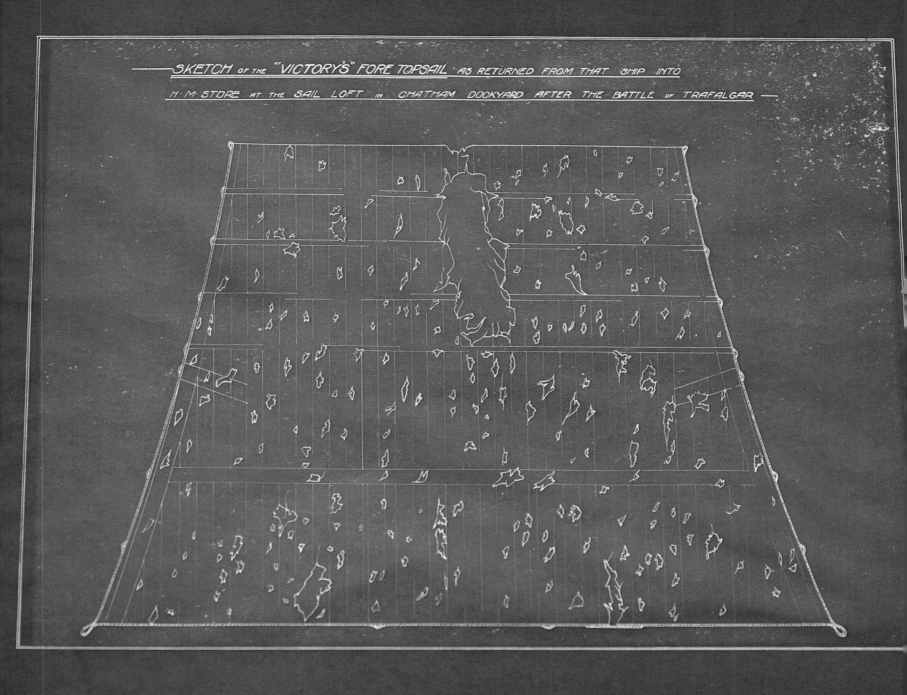

SKETCH OF THE "VICTORY'S" FORE TOPSAIL AS RETURNED FROM THAT SHIP INTO H.M. STORE AT THE SAIL LOFT IN CHATHAM DOCKYARD AFTER THE BATTLE OF TRAFALGAR —

SAIL BLUEPRINT
Plymouth Naval Base Museum, Plymouth, Devon
40cm. wide

After the Battle of Trafalgar, victorious but battered HMS *Victory* returned to the Royal Dockyard at Chatham for repairs. This blueprint shows the shot holes from just one of HMS *Victory*'s sails

The dockyard workers carefully recorded the size and position of each hole to document the ferocity of the action. The careful attention to detail shows the enormous respect the men must have felt for the fallen Nelson and his heroic crew. They labeled the sketch: "Sketch of HMS *Victory*'s Fore Topsail as returned from that ship into *HM Store* at the Sail Loft in the Chatham Dockyard after the Battle of Trafalgar."

SAIL TALLY
Chatham Historic Dockyard Museum, Chatham, Kent
94cm. long

Items of equipment in storage were often identified by means of a tally. Sails, because of their massive bulk when stored below, needed quick and sure identification. The writing on this (lower) tally faded soon after recovery. It has been replicated (above). It reads: *"Invincible* Flying Jib 26-26-6." This wooden tag provided archaeologists with the final piece of evidence needed to identify the wreck.

The numercial reference provides the sailmakers with the quantity, pattern and weight of Royal Navy canvas required to create an identical replacement or spare sail.

THESE are to Certify, That the Bearer *Lewis Christian* belonging to His Majesty's ~~Ship~~ Ship *William* N°____ was sent to this Place upon the *18* Day of *May* 1801 for Cure of *Debility* and *he not* being cured, was discharged hence this *20* of *May* 1801 to go forthwith to

out of the Service

He hath received in Cloaths
l.   s.   d.

to the Value of ———
and in Conduct Money—

Witnefs my Hand, the *20* Day of *May 1801*

Wrote to Plym
for an Extract
for the Laurel

By *Cha. Wallace*
Appointed to take Care
of Sick and Hurt Sea-
men, at *Matilda*

Printed by March and Teape, Tower-Hill, for His Majesty's Stationery Office.

Medicine and Mortality

DISABILITY DISCHARGE
Portsmouth Museum, Portsmouth, Hampshire
30cm. high

Not being cured of his "debility," this sailor was discharged from further service by the Sick and Hurt Board. Papers such as this would be carefully safeguarded, lest the owner be suspected of desertion or attract the interest of a press-gang looking for an able man to sail in His Majesty's ships.

GALLOWS NOOSE
Devonport Dockyard, Plymouth, Devon

This was yet another use for rope that was, no doubt, made on the premises. Possibly as many as 149 prisoners of war were hanged in the cavernous stone chamber that had formerly been used for treating rope with hot tar. When manila fiber came into general use at the end of the eighteenth century, it had such inherent rot resistance that the tar bath was discontinued at Plymouth.

The floor below the noose is fitted with a trap door mechanism and is said to be the last working gallows in England. One of the original wooden beams (inadvertently removed and discarded) is said to have shown a tally comprised of 149 iron nails carefully placed side-by-side as a "head count" of those who had been executed there.

Many of the French prisoners were executed after being tried and found guilty at courts-martial conducted by their own officers. There is some thought of researching the actual number of men executed by examining French naval archives. It is thought that many of the dead were routinely dumped into "lime pits" that still exist somewhere on the naval base.

CORNER of EXECUTION CHAMBER
Devonport Dockyard, Plymouth, Devon

The old hot tar chamber of The Ropery at Plymouth was fitted for its sinister new function with timbers salvaged from old ships. The massive beam that supported the noose, shown on the previous page, had been a ship's timber, and this wooden ship's grating forms part of the floor in the execution chamber.

CORNER of THE STOKE DAMEREL CHURCH GRAVEYARD
Plymouth, Devon

This corner of a church graveyard about a mile from the Devonport Dockyard was one site where lime pit burials took place. Those sailors who died in captivity or were executed might have been placed here.

At one point in the Napoleonic Wars nearly 18,000 prisoners were held around Plymouth, many in old ships that had been converted to crude prison hulks and moored in the mud-flats and backwaters. The prisoners were mainly French, but there were also numbers of Spanish, Dutch, American and Scandinavian men.

There is some record at the Devonport yards of a lime pit where bodies were disposed, but its exact location is uncertain. What is known is that only those prisoners whose families were able to pay would be given a proper funeral and a marked grave.

NAUTICAL TOMBSTONE
A Cemetery in Deal, Kent
75cm. wide

This nautical tombstone is weathered to the point of illegibility but acknowledges the gratitude the local citizens felt when area fishermen helped ferry troops across the channel to France. Out of patriotism the watermen refused to be paid.

LEAD-TOPPED AUTOPSY TABLE
Devonport Dockyard, Plymouth, Devon
2.2m. long

In the cobblestoned chamber immediately below the hangman's gallows is a single piece of furniture: a heavy wooden autopsy table with a lead top, drain and gutter. As the condemned man dropped through the gallow's trap door, he was available for internal scrutiny by the surgeons waiting below, presumably in the

SAIL CLOTH
Sail Loft, Chatham Historic Dockyard, Chatham, Kent

One of the sailmaker's grim duties aboard ship was to sew up dead sailors into their hammock for burial at sea. Bodies were weighted usually with a cannonball or two to carry them directly to the bottom of the sea.

There is a tale that some sailors would do anything, even fake their own death, to get off the ship. Therefore the sailmaker was to put one stitch, the "snitch stitch," through the sailor's nose. If the sailor were still alive, you could surely see his eyes water.

MEDICAL SYRINGE
Royal Marines Museum, Southsea, Hampshire
12.5cm. long

This surgical syringe was recovered from HMS *Invincible*. The metal is very thin and fragile. The piece in the foreground is the plunger that fits into the cylinder. The hollow needle used to inject medicine into the body is missing.

A naval surgeon was expected to report for service with a complete set of tools. The navy provided the medicines.

WOODEN FLEA COMB
Chatham Historic Dockyard Museum,
Chatham, Kent
9cm. long

With the livestock aboard, the ship's rats and the addition of pressed landsmen to the crew, fleas and lice were a constant source of irritation for all of the crew, officers and men alike. Some men tarred their long hair to keep fleas out.

SURGEON'S TOOLS
Morris Maritime Museum, Penzance, Cornwall
13cm. long

The two halves of this kit are delicately carved from animal horn. They are threaded in order to screw together to form a hollow compartment which holds an assortment of steel surgeon's blades. When the surgeon selected a blade shaped to his needs, he secured it into the broader end, and the horn case becomes the scalpel handle.

MEDICINE PHIAL from HMS Invincible
Chatham Historic Dockyard Museum, Chatham, Kent
7cm. high

Health problems were a serious concern in the eighteenth century navy. A sailor was far more likely to die from disease or accident than be killed in action. On certain stations the mortality rate was one in seven. Disease affected the officers and men alike. The surgeon often had the skill and the medicine aboard to treat many diseases successfully. Yet poxes, plagues, cholera, fevers and scurvy could rage through the ship with no effective treatment.

Although the threat of disease was real enough, there was a widespread feeling among the officers that the men were feigning illness in order to avoid work. The surgeons would frequently prescribe the drinking of seawater for suspected malingerers' "imaginary" ailments. A further incentive to keep the men working was the threat of discontinuing a man's daily alcohol rations while he was laid up.

DELFT SURGEON'S BLEEDING BOWL
Greenwich Borough Museum, Plumstead, London
19.5cm. across

Recent excavations at the old Woolwich Royal Dockyards along the Thames uncovered the surgeon's residence where this bowl was found. Bloodletting was a common practice for a whole variety of ailments at the end of the eighteenth century. Although we have come to think of bloodletting as naive or even barbaric, there is some current thought that the practice may have been beneficial in some cases, because the cut would lower the blood pressure and marshall the body's immune system.

Dress

TEXTILE/CLOTHING
Chatham Historic Dockyard Museum, Chatham, Kent
Recovered from HMS *Invincible*

Shown at left are leggings or hose that covered men's lower legs and would have been worn with breeches that came to just below the knee.

There was no standard uniform issued to seamen in the late eighteenth century. Men were frequently pressed into service and found themselves aboard ship with only the clothes they wore, and those were often ill suited for sea life. In such cases they were required to purchase a suitable outfit from the "slops room" or "slops chest" that was administered by the purser. The price of these garments could be deducted from the man's future wages. If a man died aboard ship, his clothing was auctioned off, with the proceeds going to the family of the deceased.

In situations where no suitable garments were available, men were issued light canvas or dungaree material along with needle and thread, and were ordered to fashion a wardrobe of shirts, coats, trousers, hats and other such items. Alternately, they might barter for the services of someone with sewing skills to help make their clothing.

Many chores both aloft and alow could be carried out with bare feet. As a new man became accustomed to shipboard life, he would soon begin to dress the part.

ROYAL MARINE BUTTONS
Royal Marines Museum
Southsea, Hampshire
18mm. and 25mm. wide

The pewter button on the left and the bronze button on the right are decorated with the "fouled anchor" design.

BUTTONS
Recovered from HMS *Invincible*
Chatham Historic Dockyard Museum, Chatham, Kent
Smallest is 15mm. wide, largest is 25mm. wide

"57," "39," "H" and a design featuring two shields. There are numerous examples of buttons that would have been worn by foot soldiers. The "57," for instance, may have been the 57th Regiment.

Is is by no means unusual to find evidence that foot soldiers were present on a naval ship. At the time of her loss in February of 1758, HMS *Invincible* was making haste to join a large fleet of transports and warships that had just set sail for Canada for action against the French at Louisbourg. The ship's records show that she had transported thousands of soldiers at various times.

ROYAL MARINE OFFICER'S HAT with Plumes
Royal Marines Museum, Southsea, Hampshire
60cm. across

Individual flair, rather than uniformity, often characterized military officers' mode of dress at the end of the eighteenth century. If a man had considerable wealth or a distinguished record of accomplishments, his tailoring might reflect his sense of self. Luxurious fabrics, elegantly cut, would set him apart. Fancy shoes, sashes, belts, buckles and ribbons would be combined for great effect. The hat would generally have a shape and style that indicated the owner's rank and status, but it too might be decorated to individual taste. Jewels, brocade work, feathers and ribbons were frequently used. "Bullion" was decorative material that often featured precious metallic threads (platinum or gold) woven to glittering effect.

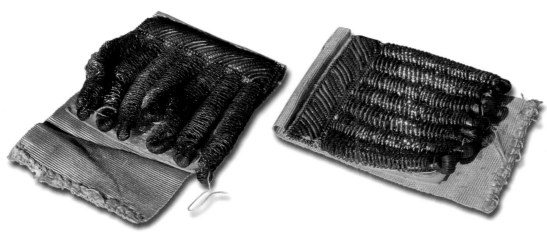

ROYAL MARINE OFFICER'S BULLION
Royal Marines Museum
Southsea, Hampshire
11cm. long

These tailor's samples of bullion date from 1790 to 1802. They could be used to decorate a marine officer's uniform coat or hat.

MARINE OFFICER'S GORGET
Royal Marines Museum, Southsea, Hampshire
12cm. wide

This marine officer's gorget is engraved with the Royal Crest and fouled anchor. It is worn as a badge or a pendant around a Royal Marine officer's neck. The base metal is copper but would have originally been gilded. The gorget is a vestigial reminder of the crucial flap of metal in a suit of armor that protected the throat at the point where the helmet and faceplate met the breastplate and body.

The marines were an integral part of the ship's company. They had sworn a special allegiance to the Crown. They were not pressed men. They were expert with small arms and trained for land actions. The lower ranks helped with ship chores like anchor retrieval, guarding the door to the captain's quarters, guarding the spirits locker and acting as an armed buffer between the ship's officers and a potentially mutinous crew. In a fierce sea battle they could replace fallen men on a gun crew.

BUCKLES
Chatham Historic Dockyard Museum, Chatham, Kent
Recovered from HMS *Invincible*
Larger buckle, 8.5cm. wide

Men wore buckles not only on their belts but on sashes across their chests and also as a decoration on their shoes. The larger buckle is stamped with the maker's name, "Turner."

FELT HAT
Recovered from HMS *Invincible*
Chatham Historic Dockyard Museum, Chatham, Kent
28cm. at widest part of brim

The curators in Chatham feel that this hat was cut down from a tricorn hat. The flat
brimmed style is similar to that worn by foot soldiers on duty in North America.

CHILD'S LEATHER SHOE
Recovered from HMS *Invincible*
Chatham Historic Dockyard Museum, Chatham, Kent
17.5cm. long

Because of its size, this almost certainly was a child's shoe. Children were sometimes known to live aboard with their parents. This child may have been part of a soldier's family being shipped overseas. Then too, ship's boys could be as young as eight years old. Nelson himself was twelve when he first went to sea. Midshipmen, who were in effect apprenticing to become officers, could be as young as ten.

ADULT SHOE
Recovered from HMS *Invincible*
Chatham Historic Dockyard Museum, Chatham, Kent
24.5cm. long

The toe of the shoe is stained with tar. Several of the shoes recovered from this wreck show wear marks of both right and left big toes in the same shoe. Foot soldiers had standing instructions to swap shoes from foot to foot once each day.

SHOE HEEL
Padstow Shipwreck Museum, Padstow, Cornwall
8cm. long

This leather heel was built up by punching diamond-shaped holes in each of several layers and pegging them with wood. No nails seem to have been used.

The shoes recovered from shipwrecks of Nelson's era are sometimes stamped "DC." This stood for "deadman's clothes." The property of the deceased was sold to benefit the widow or family.

HANDMADE TROUSERS, full view at left, detail above.
Recovered from HMS *Invincible*
Chatham Historic Dockyard Museum, Chatham, Kent

The even stitching along the seams, slash pockets and fly front show what a skilled hand could make from a piece of lightweight sailcloth. The garment shows heavy use and had been repaired in several places. It is soiled with tar and several colors of paint. The button is brass.

KNITTED WOOL MONMOUTH CAP
Recovered from HMS *Invincible*
Chatham Historic Dockyard Museum, Chatham, Kent

Since HMS *Invincible* was lost in 1758, this would almost certainly have been knitted by hand rather than machine. Close scrutiny shows a striped pattern and pom-pom. The cold and damp conditions aboard a sailing ship, taken together with depictions of shipboard life that were drawn or painted at that time, would indicate that a warm headcover was part of the sailors' everyday costume.

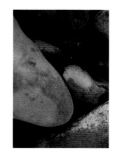

Lading and Stowage

SHINGLE

The Hard, Portsmouth, Hampshire

The beaches of southern England around Portsmouth and Portsea are often sandless and are instead covered with "shingle," small hard stones about the size of a hen's egg. As waves roll in and then retreat, it makes a rattling clatter of a sound.

This clean compact gravel has for centuries provided mariners with a handy means to ballast their ships. There is a virtually unlimited supply to be had in close proximity to one of England's greatest naval ports. It can be collected dry in barrows or buckets and deposited deep into the ship's hold. With the manpower that the navy had, huge amounts could be easily moved. In a large warship, it might fill the lower holds to a depth of eight feet or more. This extra weight would act to lower the ship's center of gravity, and act as a counter balance to the weight of the masts, sails and wind pressure. Every captain knew the ideal depth at which his ship's hull should ride in the water for maximum speed and performance.

The stowed shingle acted as "bedding" for heavy cargoes, water, spare anchors, cannon, shot and consumable stores. As a voyage progressed and situations changed, gangs of men with wooden shovels could rearrange the stones for better trim and balance. To lighten the ship in the water it could be cast overboard.

IRON "PIGS" and BALLAST STONES
The lowest hold of HMS *Victory*, Portsmouth, Hampshire

The foreground (lower left), shows blocks of iron, snugly fitted against the keel. Tons of beach shingle was laid atop this to act as bedding for the heaviest stores and provisions: enormous water and beer barrels, spare cannon and shot, gunpowder, etc. This stabilized the load and kept it from shifting as the ship pitched and rolled. As the water casks emptied they were refilled with salt water to steady the ship. As provisions were used up the shingle could be shoveled into different areas to redistribute the load.

TARRED ROPE
HMS *Victory*, Portsmouth, Hampshire

Stored in the lower hold of HMS *Victory*.

WOODEN SPADE from HMS Invincible
Royal Marines Museum, Southsea, Hampshire
92cm. long

This tool is carved from a single piece of beech. Fastener holes indicate that it was at one time fitted with an iron shoe across its front edge, to strengthen it for one of its principal uses, which was to shovel shingle. The blade of the shovel is scored with the broad arrow mark.

RUSTED IRON BLOCKS
HMS *Trincomalee*, Hartlepool, Teesside
Approximately 1m. long and 20cm. at the widest part

These heavy iron "pigs" are the primary ballast in HMS *Trincomalee*. The 1820 frigate is currently undergoing a major refit and is in drydock, so these weights are stacked in the hold to allow access to the planking below them. In their normal position, they would be laid like paving bricks along the keel to provide a low center of gravity and act as a counter balance to wind and wave action, and keep the vessel "on an even keel." The dimensions of the pigs were standardized, including the position of the holes, which allowed the insertion of iron "staples" that could be used to interlock the blocks.

Anchors

RUSTED ANCHOR
Chatham Historic Dockyard, Chatham, Kent
Over 3m. long

This anchor is at the end of its working life. The ship's anchor is subjected to rough service. It can be dropped to the bottom and land on rock. It is expected to hold a ship's thousands of tons safely.

The anchorsmiths would sometimes be asked to forge a giant bower anchor of "seventy hundred-weight," about three and one half tons. Such work could only be carried out in the spring and fall. In the summer the heat from the "smithery" was unbearable, and in the cold of winter, the iron couldn't be brought up to the required temperatures.

Anchorsmiths were among the highest paid men in the dockyards. Most men could simply not bear the searing heat of the forge.

RUSTED IRON ANCHOR
Chatham Historic Dockyard, Chatham, Kent
3m. long

The broken and aging anchor is showing the laminations of the smith's welds. The iron is wrought in such a way as to exploit the tough, sinewy "grain" structure in the forged metal that has been compared to that of hickory wood.

CATHEAD
HMS *Victory*, Portsmouth, Hampshire

The end of the stout timber projecting out from HMS *Victory*'s bow is decorated with a carved and gilded crown. The cathead was often carved with a cat or lion's head, which presumably frightened away wharf rats.

As the massive iron anchor is brought up from the bottom and gets closer to the hull, there is the danger that the flukes could damage the side of the ship, especially in rough waters. The cathead allows this operation to be carried out a short distance away from the ship's side.

A special tackle is fastened to the ring of the anchor and it is "fished and catted" (brought up and secured) in its riding position on the bow.

The black loop of rope that holds the anchor to the cathead is the "stopper." This could simply be cut through to drop the anchor. The main anchor cable is bent onto the ring. The ring itself has been wrapped in cord as an anti-chafing measure called "puddening."

CATHEAD CARVING
Falmouth Maritime Museum, Falmouth, Cornwall
40cm. wide

"Cathead of HMS *Foudroyant*. Presented by Mr. Wheatley Cobb." There were two ships of that name. One was Nelson's flagship during his service in the Mediterranean Fleet. The other, HMS *Foudroyant*, is the frigate now being restored in Hartlepool. She had reverted to her original name, HMS *Trincomalee*.

ANCHOR CABLE
HMS *Victory*, Portsmouth, Hampshire
62cm. in circumference

Shown above are sections of HMS *Victory*'s massive anchor cable. The anchor alone could weigh 7000 pounds. The weight of the cable itself plus the strain of the ship against the seabed took a tremendous human effort to break the anchor free and get it aboard. Over 100 men at one time straining at the wooden bars inserted into the capstan for hours might succeed in bringing a few yards of cable aboard. Often on a ship-of-the-line the capstan was manned by the marines.

Parts of the cable above show where it has been "wormed." A rope of much smaller circumference has been spiraled along the larger rope. This would keep muck and marine growth from becoming embedded in the deep grooves and make handling a bit easier.

THE MESSENGER
HMS *Victory*, Portsmouth, Hampshire
23cm. in circumference

The anchor cable referred to at the left was so large and cumbersome that it could not be directly wrapped around the capstan during retrieval of the anchor. Instead, the "messenger," shown at right, a much smaller cable, was rigged around the capstan in a continuous loop, and the larger cable was fastened to it by a series of short temporary ropes called "nips." As the efforts of the men working the capstan brought the anchor cable aboard, it was the job of the ship's boys to remove the nips at the after end and retie them forward. They of course became known as the "little nippers."

Fire and Water

PUMP BOX

The very lowest point in the hold of HMS *Victory*, Portsmouth, Hampshire

Channels for bilge water called limber passages ran fore and aft on either side of the "keelson." The keelson (sometimes "kelson") runs inside the ship parallel to the keel, to which it is bolted. Together, these timbers constitute the longitudinal "spine" of the ship. The gutter thus formed channeled bilge water to a collecting well near the base of the main mast. A chain-driven pump manned by several men could move a ton of water in a few minutes. As with firefighting, it was part of the battle plan that designated men from the gun crew could be deployed to pump duty if the ship was taking on water.

The massive beam crossing the keelson is called a rider. Originally, it would have have been hand sawn from oak. In this view it measures twenty inches in thickness. Damage reports after the Battle of Trafalgar indicte that several of HMS *Victory*'s riders were "shot through and broke" by enemy cannon fire.

LEAD DRAIN STRAINER
Recovered from HMS *Invincible*
Chatham Historic Dockyard Museum, Chatham, Kent
20cm. square

In spite of its heavy weight, lead was easily worked into various shapes and was used in conjunction with pumps, dales, scuppers, gutters and other plumbing devices to direct the flow of water around the ship.

BRAKE PUMP
Chatham Historic Dockyard Museum
Chatham, Kent
40cm. wide

This is the "head" of a suction pump known as a brake pump. Although HMS *Invincible's* main pump was chain operated, brake pumps were more useful for fire fighting, as they could deliver water under pressure. This pump may have been part of HMS *Invincible's* own equipment or could have been put on board in an attempt to salvage her after she hit the sand bank.

The elm head was wrapped with a leather gasket that formed a flexible seal, as it rode up and down in the pump's cylinder. The leather flap mechanism acted as a valve.

ELM TREE PUMP
HMS *Victory*, Portsmouth, Hampshire
29cm. diameter

Shown is a section of HMS *Victory's* original "elm tree pump." Sections of elm logs were hollowed out and joined together to form a pipe. This extended from the upper deck straight down into the ship, with the lower end piercing the hull. Thus seawater could be drawn up for firefighting, bathing or any other use that could conserve the precious fresh water. Elm was a wood particularly suited to those fittings and parts of the ship that were constantly wet.

LEATHER BUCKET

HMS *Invincible*, Chatham Historic Dockyard Museum
Chatham, Kent
25cm. high

HMS *Invincible* was a heavily armed "third-rate" ship of seventy-four guns. The battle plan provided for designated men from each gun crew to take up firefighting duty if needed. Buckets such as this were placed throughout the ship and filled with salt water. In fighting a major fire a hand-to-hand bucket brigade would form to pass the water along.

This sturdy example is made of cow's hide and is stamped with a "hide mark" to the left of the seam near the top rim that shows the royal seal of George II. The bright stitching along the seams is all original. The handle had become detached. A hoop of hazelwood is stitched into the top of the bucket to keep it round. The bottom of the bucket is branded with a broad arrow.

EIGHTEENTH CENTURY CANDLE LAMP

Plymouth Naval Base Museum, Plymouth, Devon
45cm. tall with handle

It was very dark below decks. Concern about fire and gunpowder explosion put severe restrictions on every open flame: galley fires, lighting and smoking. This sturdy lamp is hinged at the shoulders to install the candle, and the lid at top slides up to form a chimney to vent heat and smoke. A lantern was considered an essential tool at each gun station.

Officers

The GREAT STERN WINDOWS of HMS Victory
Portsmouth, Hampshire

At Trafalgar the top tier would have been Admiral Hardy's day cabin below that was Nelson's apartment. Twenty-seven window sashes, each with nine "lights," or panes, are shown, and there is not a single right angle in one of them. In preparing for battle the windows sashes were removed and sent below, as was the officers' furniture. Guns pointing aft that were always kept in place were run out. Removable bulkheads (walls) and room dividers were sent below to clear the fighting decks for the length of the ship.

There was often a good deal of time to prepare for battle as two ships manevered toward the encounter. It was sometimes the case that items belonging to the senior officers such as desks, tables, chairs and cabinets would be put over the side of the ship in unmanned "furniture boats" to be towed or cast loose for retrieval after the battle. Conversely, these same fine possessions might be thrown overboard in haste to clear the decks for an imminent battle.

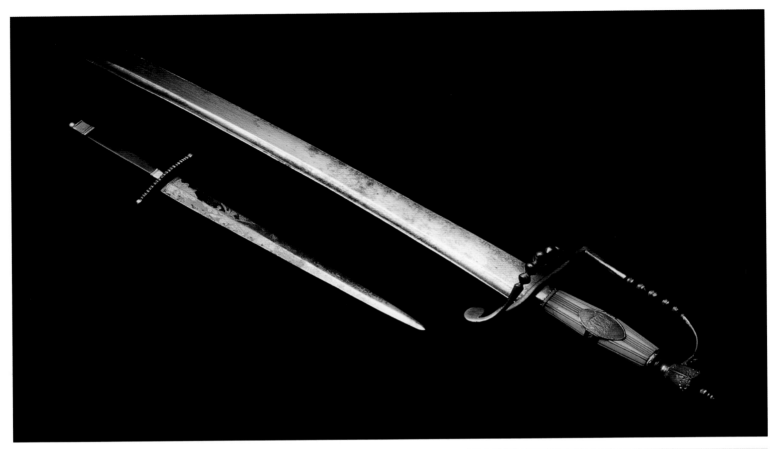

ADMIRAL SIR JOHN HINDEMARSH'S SWORD *and* DIRK

Hartlepool Historic Quay Museum, Hartlepool, Teesside
Sword length 78.5cm., blade length 63cm., blood gutter 48cm.
Dirk length 33cm., blade length 23cm.

This sword belonged to John Hindemarsh who went to sea as a cabin boy and went on to become a knighted rear admiral and the first governor-General of South Australia. An inventory of Admiral Sir John's belongings refers to this weapon as "five ball Spradoon." The "five ball" nomenclature refers to the decoration of the knuckle-guard. The dirk, or dagger, shows fancy engraving and "gold on blue" coloration. Highlights of the Admiral's long career, including a decoration for service in the Battle of Trafalgar, are found on the opposite page.

DOCKYARD SWORD, detail

Rochester Guildhall Museum, Rochester, Kent
94cm. from pommel to tip

The brass "half-basket" knuckle-guard, which is decorated with a fouled anchor, extends up into the jaws of the Royal Crown lion, which is the pommel decoration. The grip of dogfish skin has the texture of sandpaper to resist slipping. It would have been carried by an officer assigned to the security force at the Royal Dockyard at Chatham.

NAVAL GENERAL SERVICE MEDAL, front and back views
Hartlepool Historic Quay Museum, Hartlepool, Teesside

The Naval General Service Medal was introduced in 1848. Bars representing 200 actions between 1793 and 1815 could be attached to the ribbon. This medal belonged to Admiral Sir John Hindemarsh who earned seven bars. The bars honor an illustrious and courageous naval career. The earliest action hangs at the bottom, the most recent is at the top.

> Java
> Basque Roads, 1809
> Trafalgar
> Gut of Gibraltar, July 12, 1801
> Nile
> 17 June 1795
> 1 June 1794

At just eleven years of age John Hindemarsh (1782-1860), saw his first duty at sea on HMS *Bellerophon*. The sailors called her the "Billy Ruffian." This is the same ship that years later helped transport the vanquished Napoleon Bonaparte to his final exile on St. Helena.

As Hindemarsh's long career progressed and he rose through the command ranks to rear admiral, he was also knighted. The ships he sailed, listed chronologically, were:

> *1793* HMS *Bellerophon*
> *1800* HMS *Spencer*
> *1803* HMS *Victory*
> *1803* HMS *Phoebe*
> *1805* HMS *Beagle*
> *1809* HMS *Nisus*
> *1830* HMS *Scylla*
> *1836* HMS *Buffalo*

PRINT
"The Evening Before the Battle of Copenhagen"
Thomas Davidson, painter; from author's collection

Horatio Nelson was second in command of a strong squadron of ships under Sir Hyde Parker. During the heated battle, Hyde Parker, fearing that Nelson was in danger of being overpowered, signaled Nelson's ship to break off action. When the signal was brought to Nelson's attention, he put the telescope to his sightless eye and exclaimed to his flag captain, "You know I really do not see the signal."

The artist has taken care to render the details of the scene with a great deal of accuracy regarding dress, table service and even the officers and steward who were known to have been present. The one area where he has taken license is in the generous amount of head room he has provided above the men.

Naval custom permitted the royal toast, "The King, God Bless Him" to be offered while seated aboard ship, because of the confined space.

CHAMBER POT
Royal Marines Museum, Southsea, Hampshire
22cm. across

This chamber pot, decorated with a floral design, was found in an excavation of an officer's quarters in Southsea. It was made in Germany near Cologne.

GENTLEMAN'S WIG CURLER
Chatham Historic Dockyard Museum, Chatham, Kent
6cm. long

This item, made of pipe clay, was found among the wreckage of HMS *Invincible*.

The relatively few ship's officers were quartered astern, depending on their rank. An officer might enjoy the comfort of a cot, a few pieces of furniture and possibly a window to provide light and ventilation. If his rank and station allowed, he might have had the services of a personal steward or even a small staff of servants to tend to his needs.

Powdered wigs were worn as a matter of proper fashion. Dozens of such curlers made of pipe clay were found on the wreckage of HMS *Invincible*. This example is even marked with the owner's initials: "W.B.". A list of all the commissioned officers that had served on HMS *Invincible* shows just two officers, both lieutenants, with those initials. A William Bayne served aboard until November 1756 and a William Brown was serving aboard at the time of her loss.

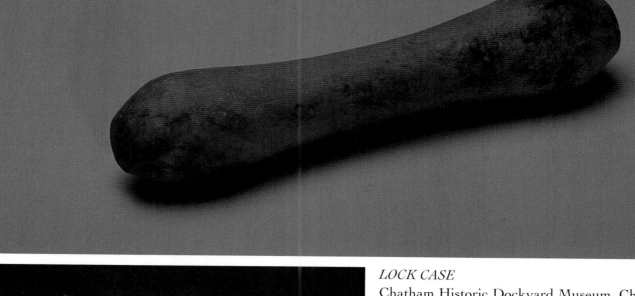

LOCK CASE
Chatham Historic Dockyard Museum, Chatham, Kent
17.5cm.

One of several identical brass lock cases found on HMS *Invincible*. The doorknob is missing. When mounted on the inside of a door, the lock could be secured by sliding the switch on the bottom left. In this position the door could not be opened from the outside without a key.

Gunpowder

GLASS CUPBOARD DOORS
HMS *Trincomalee*, Jackson Dock, Hartlepool, Teesside

This is the Lantern Cupboard on the outside wall of the Powder-Handling room. The HMS *Trincomalee* is currently undergoing an extensive refit. If she were in commission with a Royal Navy crew, the glass would no doubt be shiny bright. There were several such cupboards around the room.

Most of the walls (bulkheads) below decks were painted white to make the most of what little light there was. The light from the candles or lanterns placed inside would be cast through a thick polished glass lens, or "glim," shown on the following page, to provide light in rooms where gunpowder was handled.

The tons of gunpowder carried on a warship were stored with the greatest care in special rooms deep in the center part of the ship where they would be least vulnerable known as the powder magazine. In battle there was often a separate room for "handling" or "filling" separate from the bulk storage area. Here cartridges would be measured out and prepared to be carried up to the gundeck. Every caution was taken to prevent even the simplest spark from touching off disaster. Brass tools were used to open the barrels. Brass, wood or lead was used for scoops, cups and measures to prevent sparks.

The room was virtually wrapped in a one-inch-thick canvas or felt blanket that was soaked with seawater. The opening where the crew could enter was draped with woolen tassels which would brush up against the seaman to discharge static electricity.

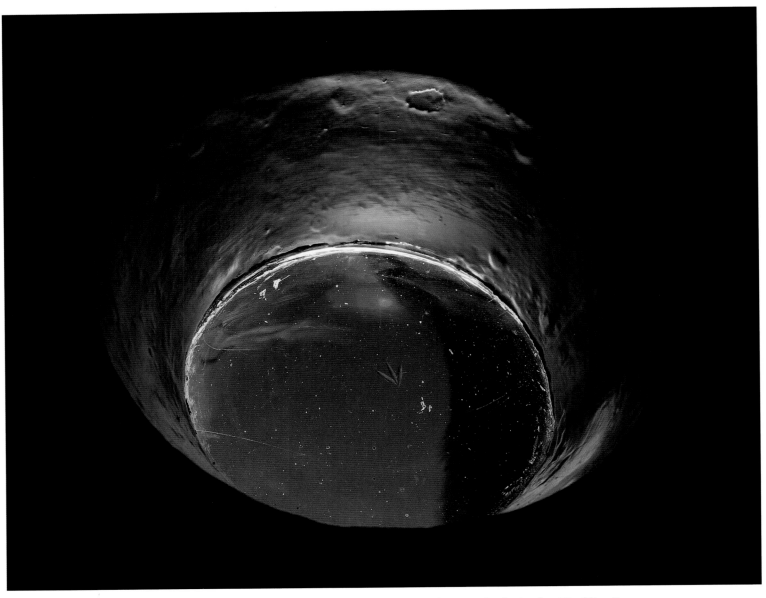

GLIM, from inside the Powder-Handling Room
HMS *Trincomalee*, Jackson Dock, Hartlepool, Teesside
Previous page gives view from outside the Powder-Handling Room.
13cm. wide

This thick glass window was curved in a bulls eye design to form a lens and direct as much of the lantern's light as possible into the room. The heat from the candle lantern is thus kept safely on the opposite side of the wall.

In order to mark it as government property, the glass is etched with the broad arrow.

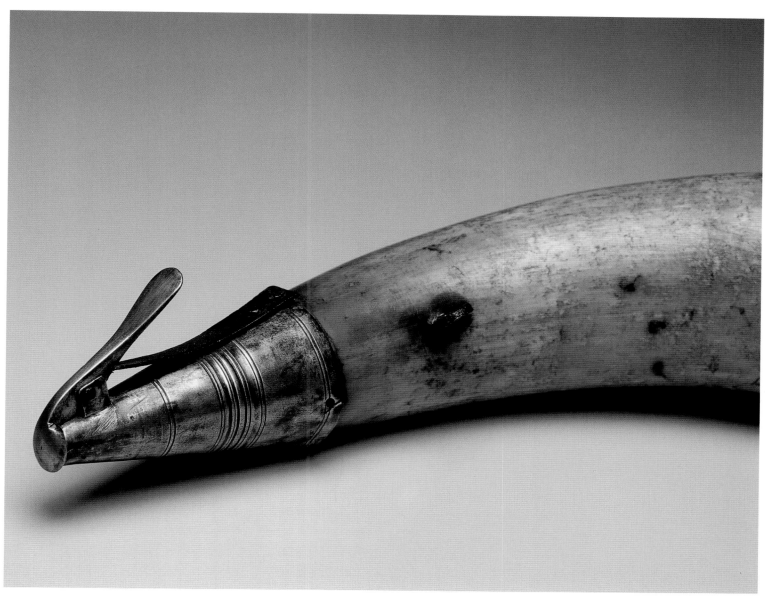

POWDER HORN from HMS Mars, *(detail of brass pouring spout)*
Rochester Guildhall Museum, Rochester, Kent
33cm. overall length

The Board of Ordnance had gunpowder manufacturing mills at Faversham and Waltham Abbey. The Royal Arsenal at Woolwich had laboratories for testing gunpowder.

The standard recipe was seventy-five parts saltpeter, ten parts sulphur and five parts charcoal. It could be formulated "L.G." (large grain), which burned more slowly for use in cannon, or "F.G." (fine grain), used for small arms and priming powder for cannons. Great care was taken at each step: manufacture, delivery, and loading aboard the ship. Loading the barrels of gunpowder was often the very last

chore before a ship set sail. A ship loaded with powder was especially vulnerable to fire, accident or treachery any time it was in port or near land. At provisioning yards the gunpowder was warehoused and loaded far from all other ships and buildings.

This powder horn was used aboard HMS *Mars*, which fought at Trafalgar. It would have held the fine-grained powder that primed the touch hole of the cannon in order to send the spark down into the main charge.

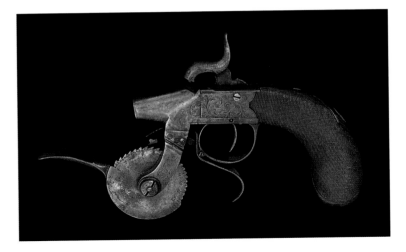

PROVING PISTOL
Hartlepool Historic Quay Museum, Hartlepool, Teesside
32cm. long

This little instrument is not a weapon in that it does not fire a shot. Instead, it was used to provide a comparative measurement of the explosive power for a particular batch of gunpowder. A carefully measured amount of a known powder was fired, and the reading on the toothed wheel was noted, then an equal amount of new powder was used and the readings could be compared.

It was often referred to by its French name *éprouvette* from the verb *éprouver*, "to test." In French *éprouvette* is also the word for "test tube."

The hammer on this device shows that it was a percussion type of lock, which was an improvement of the flintlock. The percussion lock started to come into general use around 1820.

LEAD LINED POT
Padstow Shipwreck Museum, Padstow, Cornwall
11cm. across

This lead-lined copper pot was used as a measure or a scoop for handling gunpowder. Lead and copper were chosen to prevent sparks.

GUNPOWDER BALANCE SCALE
Plymouth Naval Base Museum, Plymouth, Devon
Balance bar is 60cm. across

This finely made balance scale is marked "1752-Vandome, Titfords and Pawson." The trays are copper, the chains and balance mechanism are brass.

For a substance that has only three basic ingredients, gunpowder could be formulated in many ways, and quality could vary enormously. A first-rate ship of the line like HMS *Victory* might sail with thirty tons carefully stored in her magazines. It was of utmost importance to provide the gun crews with the precise quantity and ideal quality for their particular weapon.

Testing was carried out constantly, and at every level: at the government's own powder mills, by captains who took on fresh supplies (often in foreign ports) and by gunners and gun crews who actually fought the ship.

Leisure, Crafts and Recreation

SCRIMSHAW
Hartlepool Historic Quay Museum, Hartlepool, Teesside
8.5cm. wide

The "scrimshander" has executed his warship design by scratching into the polished whale's tooth with a needle. Later, black ink was rubbed into the scratches. The piece is initialed and dated "J.W. 1797."

In spite of the never-ending series of chores that a sailor was required to perform aboard ship, there were countless hours over the weeks and months where he was left to his own amusement. The many examples of hand crafts that survive show that many sailors would busy themselves with the most intricate and detailed creations. The projects were usually small and could be easily tucked in with their belongings when they were not being worked. The shipboard skills of sail making, repair and ropework could be expressed as needlepoint design, leather craft or construction of their own clothing.

KEYS with HEAVING KNOT DECORATION
Hartlepool Historic Quay Museum, Hartlepool, Teesside
The single key above is 9cm. long.

To get a line from ship to ship or from ship to shore, a heaving line would sometimes be used. This would be a light line that was finished on one end with a heaving-knot, or "monkey's fist," that was formed with a slug of lead in the center for weight. This line would be used to pull heavier ropes across the span.

The head of the small key is wrapped in the same distinctive style as the ring attached to the ship's anchor. The anti-chafing rope wrapping, as noted earlier, is called puddening.

ROPE DICE SHAKER *with* BONE *or* IVORY DICE
Hartlepool Historic Quay Museum, Hartlepool, Teesside
8.5cm. wide

The shaker is a version of the turk's head knot.

WOODEN DICE SHAKER
Hartlepool Historic Quay Museum, Hartlepool, Teesside
8cm. tall

Gambling was officially forbidden, and must have been the most universally broken rule. Sailors loved to gamble. The stakes could be money, alcohol, tobacco, chores, or personal services such as laundry. The dice are made of boxwood. The shaker's decorative base is woven from cotton marline.

SAILOR'S CLAY PIPE
Hartlepool Historic Quay Museum, Hartlepool, Teesside
8.5cm. long

Tobacco was supplied as a regular part of the men's rations. Open flame was forbidden on most of the ship, so chewing tobacco was common. At certain times, areas of the ship were designated for smoking.

SHELL DESIGN MIRROR
Hartlepool Historic Quay Museum
Hartlepool, Teesside
12cm. long

This mirror decorated with tiny seashells was made by someone who had both the time and the sensitivity to create something beautiful with material found in the mudflats and on the beach.

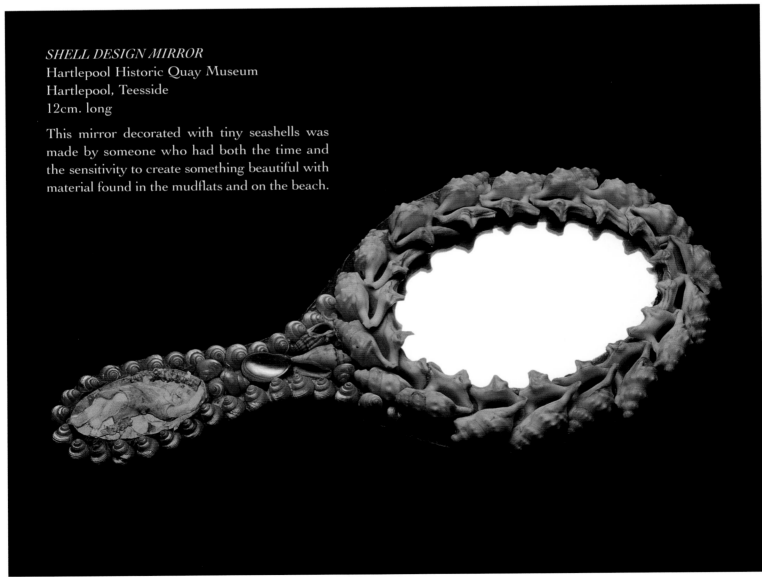

WOODEN GAME BOARD
Chatham Historic Dockyard Museum, Chatham Kent
20cm. long

This wooden game board was found on HMS *Invincible*. The game was called "Old Fox" and is similar to a modern game called "Fox and Geese." It would originally have had game pieces (or colored pebbles) representing two foxes and twenty geese.

DECORATED BOTTLE
Hartlepool Historic Quay Museum
Hartlepool, Teesside
16cm. tall

This glass bottle is decorated with basketware and a sailor's fancy ropework.

Ship Construction and Repair

MAST HOUSE
Chatham Historic Dockyard, Chatham, Kent

The Mast House and Mould Loft at the Chatham Dockyard dates from 1753. It is in this building that old ship timbers were found in the 1990s. The building has been put to many uses over the centuries. It is thought that the patterns used to create HMS *Victory*'s original lines were "laid down" on the floor of the upper lofts.

At one point in the early 1800s in a time of peace, scores of masts and spars of decommissioned warships were stored here out of the weather.

DUSTY SHIP'S TIMBERS and HAMMOCK RAIL
Chatham Historic Dockyard, Chatham, Kent

When workers recently lifted up the floorboards in the old Mast House (shown on the previous page) at the Chatham Historic Dockyard, they discovered hundreds of ship's timbers that had been removed from an eighteenth century ship that was either broken up or undergoing a major refit. The curators are hopeful that after studying the curves, scarfs and angles they may be able to determine the size and rig of the vessel (or vessels) that now lies in pieces. It is even possible that they will uncover some clue as to the actual identity.

One example of the valuable information that the site has already yielded is lying in the dusty space between the two deck timbers. There is a long slender batten lying along the beam on the right that is called a hammock rail. It would have been nailed into the overhead beams on the gundeck where the men lived.

Each sailor would sling his hammock between two such rails for sleeping; at other times the hammock would be bundled and stowed elsewhere. Later ships have iron hooks for hammocks, and this is one of the few, perhaps the only, wooden example to survive. A simple detail like this can be used to surmise how closely the men were cramped together.

Markings on this hammock rail confirm that only 35cm. of width was allowed to each sleeping sailor. "Stealing a man's space" was a flogging offense.

EIGHT-INCH NAILS
Greenwich Borough Museum, Plumstead, London

Lest these heavy, hand-forged spikes be used for private constructions, they have been marked as government property with the broad arrow.

COMPASS TIMBER
Chatham Historic Dockyard, Chatham, Kent

When the shipwright's plans called for curved beams, the ideal would be to saw them from naturally curved tree formations, or "compass timber." With such bench marks as "80 acres of mature oak to build a '74" or "2000 trees to build a ship-of-the-line" it is easy to see that England's native supply would run short.

The longitudinal cracks called "checking" shown in these old timbers are natural and don't affect the strength of the piece.

CAULKER'S TOOLS
Falmouth Maritime Museum, Falmouth, Cornwall

The chisel-like caulking iron pictured above is 15cm. long. As simple as pounding oakum fibers into the seams with a mallet and iron might appear, the caulker was in fact expert at waterproofing all of the ship's surfaces: hull, decks, roofs, windows and skylights.

CAULKING IRON

Recovered from HMS *Invincible*, Chatham Historic Dockyard Museum, Chatham, Kent
20cm. long

Caulking the ship to keep her seams watertight was an important and highly skilled craft. The caulker's tool box had an assortment of specifically designed irons for wedging oakum into the cracks. This one was called a triple crease iron or chintzing iron.

CARVED WOODEN DECORATIONS;
PAINTED OAK LEAF, ACORN
and FLORAL ROSETTE
Plymouth Naval Base Museum, Plymouth, Devon
The oak leaf is 22.5cm. long.

Once a tiny bit of filigree on a huge ship, now these carved figures may be all that remain.

FLOWERS, CARVED and PAINTED
Plymouth Naval Base Museum, Plymouth, Devon
86.3cm. long

This piece, carved from a single plank, once decorated a warship's bow quarter-boards, as an accent to the main figure head.

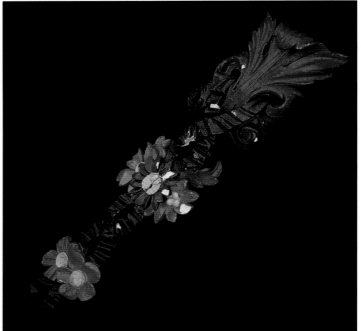

ROYAL CYPHER
Plymouth Naval Base Museum, Plymouth, Devon
60cm. high

This superbly made Royal Cypher of King George III is stamped with the date 1817, which was just three years before he died. The bolt holes for mounting would indicate that it was displayed in such a way that it could be viewed from either side, as in an arch above a doorway. It is forged of bronze in several pieces and keyed and pinned together rather than simply cast as a single unit.

BATTLE HONORS WON at USHANT, 1778
Plymouth Naval Base Museum, Plymouth, Devon
65cm. wide, painted carved wood

"Ushant" is a French island off the western tip of Brittany known as "Finisterre" (Land's End). The French refer to the island as "L'île d'Ouessant." Its rocky shoals, frequently shrouded by dense fog, have caused hundreds of shipwrecks. Countless sea battles have also taken place in the surrounding waters.

The warship that earned and then proudly displayed this decoration is not known. The honors bestowed on a vessel and her crew can carry over when a new ship with the same name replaces her.

WOODEN OVAL with UNION FLAG
Plymouth Naval Base Museum, Plymouth, Devon
68cm. across

It's a sad moment in a ship's life when she has lived out her usefulness and is sent to the breaker's yard. It must have been especially sad for those who built the ship, sailed in her and possibly fought on her decks.

Recycling is not a new practice, and the ship would be stripped of anything useful. Masts, guns, steering gear, blocks and hundreds of other pieces of gear were often pulled off and might see use in another vessel.

The few decorative items that a warship displayed, such as the ships bow figure, stern carvings and battle honors, were often salvaged at the last minute as a keepsake or a sign of respect.

HMS INVINCIBLE'*s SHIPS TIMBER with TRENAIL*
Chatham Historic Dockyard Museum, Chatham, Kent
74cm. long

This small ship's timber shows a partly fitted trenail. Thousands of these round pegs were used as nails to hold the hull timbers together and to secure the planking. They had an advantage over metal nails or spikes in that they didn't rust and the shipwright could continue to shape the timber after they had been fitted. A trenail is sometimes notched at the end to allow a wedge to be driven into it for a snug fit.

WOODEN FRAGMENT and BRONZE BOLT
Padstow Shipwreck Museum, Padstow, Cornwall
10cm. across

Sailors often speak proudly of a stout ship as "oak built and bronze fastened." These two elements are still clinging to each other even after the shipwreck of HMS *Primrose* took them to the bottom in 1809.

INTERNAL HULL
HMS *Victory*, Portsmouth, Hampshire

This is HMS *Victory*'s internal hull structure at the "turn of the bilge," well below the waterline. The triple-planked construction is 60cm. (2 feet) thick. The massive oak rib, or "frame," is also about 60cm. thick at the lower end.

COPPER BOLT and ROVE
HMS *Victory*, Portsmouth, Hampshire
The bolt is 2.5cm in diameter.

This copper bolt and rove (a kind of washer) is standing proud of the keelson on HMS *Victory*. This fastener would normally lie flush with the massive internal twenty-foot oak timber as it grips the floor timber below it. Because the ship currently rests in drydock in Portsmouth, the wood has dried out and contracted by just this much.

TOMBSTONE
Graveyard, Rochester, Kent
70cm. tall

"In Memory of David Greenfield Gordon Watt Shipwright and Lamented Son of David and Sarah Watt and Native of Southwick In the County of Durham Who Fell from the Brig West Kent of and at Dorchester and was Unfortunately Drowned." As shipwright he was probably a dockyard worker and not part of the ship's company.

CARVED POST

HMS *Trincomalee*, Hartlepool, Teesside
17.5cm. diameter at widest part

This "twisted barley" design is a signature detail of the Wadia Shipbuilding Yards in Bombay, India. It is part of the companionway railing.

The First Lord of the Admiralty, Lord St.Vincent, was concerned with the serious shortage of timber in England (a ship-of-the-line required up to 2000 mature oaks). He directed that some ships be built of teak in the yards of the East India Company. Work on HMS *Trincomalee* began in 1816.

The durable qualities of Malabar teak are evident. HMS *Trincomalee*'s crew proudly proclaims the distinction of "The Oldest British Warship Afloat." Malabar teak is strong, beautiful and rot resistant and earns Lloyds of London's highest rating for wood shipbuilding material.

The shipyards in England were so concerned with the loss of jobs to foreign yards that the shipwrights in Chatham spread the rumor that teak "splinters" were poisonous. This refers not so much to a little nick on the finger but the horrible wood shrapnel splinters that sailors suffered when a cannonball hits the ship.

PAINTED "F" GRAPHIC

HMS *Trincomalee*, Hartlepool, Teesside
30cm. across

This is the "head" of the steering mechanism below deck in the stern of HMS *Trincomalee*. It obviously dates from the period when the frigate was known as HMS *Foudroyant*. The bright decoration and padding serve to remind any sailor working nearby that the massive timber swings with great power as the ship tacks or rides in rough seas.

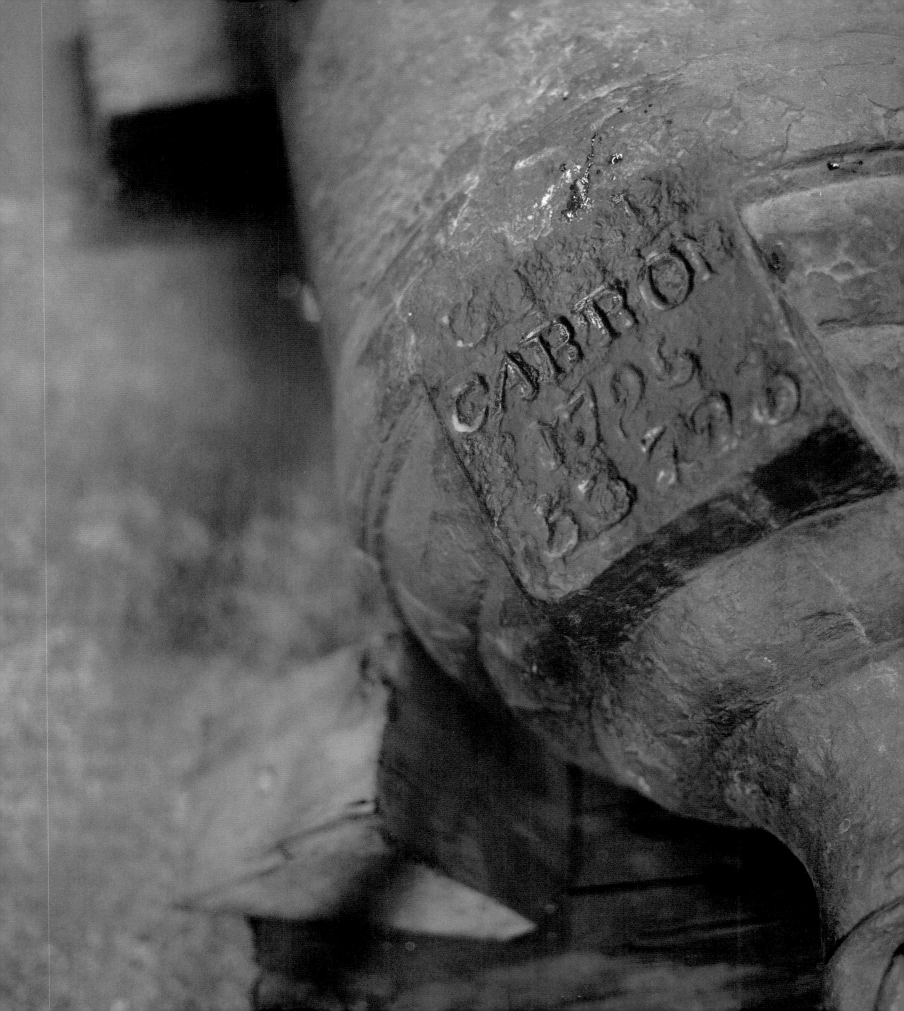

Cannons

CARRONADE, "THE SMASHER"
Ordnance Gallery, Chatham Historic Dockyard, Chatham, Kent

Shown at left is the foundry mark of the Carron Company of Falkirk, Scotland, hence the name "carronade." Nelson had two of the largest carronades aimed forward as "bow chasers" on HMS *Victory* at Trafalgar.

The stubby little barrel hurled a sixty-eight-pound projectile. The guns were credited with being very effective early in that battle. They were considered by some to be an experimental weapon, and often were not included in the official count of the ship's guns. Exclusive of the gun carriage, each 68 pounder weighed 3600 pounds. Instead of a "button" at the breech end, we can see that the carronade is bored through to form a ring, which would have held an elevating screw for aiming.

HOWITZER from HMS PRIMROSE, *two views above*
Padstow Shipwreck Museum, Padstow, Cornwall
Bore diameter: 90mm. Weight: 125kg.

This small cannon or howitzer was recovered from the underwater wreckage of the eighteen-gun brig HMS *Primrose* (built at Fowey, Cornwall, by the Nicholls Shipbuilders in 1802). The museum curators have determined that the foundry that made this brass deck gun was in Denmark.

HMS *Primrose* sailed from Portsmouth on the fourteenth of January in 1809 and wrecked off the point of land called "The Lizard" in Cornwall on the twenty-second of the same month.

BAR SHOT form AMERICAN VESSEL, below
Hull Museum, Kingston-upon-Hull, Yorkshire
27cm. long

This bar shot washed up on, English coast in the days following American Captain John Paul Jones' defeat of the British HMS *Serapis* in 1779 within sight of land off Flamborough Head, not far from Hull. HMS *Serapis* struck her colors in surrender and Jones brought his men aboard his captured prize as his own vessel, the *Bon Homme Richard* was sinking. Earlier in this fierce battle, during a lull in the action, the British captain demanded: "Have you struck your colors?" John Paul Jones answered, "I have not yet begun to fight."

Upon being fired from a cannon, this cast-iron projectile would tumble in flight. It was designed to damage sails, spars and rigging.

GUN CARRIAGE
Ordnance Gallery, Chatham Historic Dockyard
Chatham, Kent

The great weight of the cannon is balanced approximately at the trunnions, the cylindrical castings projecting out from the barrel. The powder charge and the shot are rammed all the way into the barrel, which, of course, affected the gun's balance. The wooden handspike rests on the stepped side-rail of the carriage and lifts the cannon's enormously heavy breech end for aiming. The quoin is the wedge with handle that can be slid in place to hold the gun at the desired elevation. The gun carriage played an important part in gun accuracy.

This replica was built at the Ordnance Workshop at Chatham. The wheels, or "trucks," are fitted with iron tires. These would have damaged the ships deck and would not have been used at sea. The lower surface of the handspike is shod with a strip of leather to keep it from chipping away at the carriage, affecting accuracy. The iron rings allow the attachment of "breeching tackle," the system of ropes and pulleys used to run the gun in and out and absorb the recoil during firing.

CANNONBALL RACKS
HMS *Trincomalee*, Hartlepool, Teesside

A supply of solid, cast-iron cannonballs was a considerable weight in a wooden ship. A frigate such as HMS *Trincomalee* had "shot lockers" in the after hold, just aft of the mainmast, where much of the iron could be stored (low and close to the centerline of the ship.

These shot racks are along the "carpenter's walk" which was a narrow passage designed to give the ship's carpenter access to repair shot holes dangerously near the waterline in battle.

Similar racks were located throughout the ship to store shot as close as possible to each of HMS *Trincomalee*'s forty-six guns.

Some discrepancy exists about the number of guns HMS *Trincomalee* would have mounted were she put into immediate service. She was built as peace broke out, and stored "in ordinary." For her subsequent service she was armed according to the needs at that time.

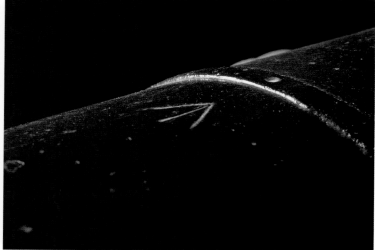

BRONZE CANNON SIGHT, above left
Morris Maritime Museum, Penzance, Cornwall
20cm. long

A cannon's accuracy was largely determined by the skill and experience of her gun crew and not upon mechanical technology. This rather crude device would be mounted along the barrel and provide a reference angle from one firing to the next.

CANNON on HMS Victory, *detail, above right*
Portsmouth, Hampshire

The broad arrow mark on the barrel of a cannon was put on not necessarily at the time it was made but at the time that it had been successfully test fired, or "proved." Proving a gun was done by charging the gun with considerably more powder and shot than a normal load. Double powder, double shot is an oversimplification, but the exact formula might be close to this. The load would be carefully measured by weight.

If a gun had been out of service, stored away or even recovered from a shallow wreck site it would have to be proved again to assure its safety, suitability and accuracy. After test firings, if it measured up to the standards, it could be marked with an additional broad arrow and returned to service.

DECK RING, left
HMS *Victory*, Portsmouth, Hampshire

A system of blocks (pulleys) and tackle (ropes, hooks, rings, etc.) was needed at each cannon in order to run the gun out into firing position, run it in to reload or catch the backward recoil as the gun is fired. Deck rings such as this, as well as rings fastened into the bulkheads along the gunports, provided a secure anchor for the tackle to hook into.

TAMPION and WAD
Padstow Shipwreck Museum, Padstow, Cornwall

The "tompion" (also spelled tampion) on the right is made of pine. In its original condition it was a single piece of solid wood tapering down to 13cm. to plug the muzzle of a 24-pounder when the gun was not in use. Both the tompion and the wad next to it were recovered from the wreck of HMS *Invincible*.

The wad is composed of recycled rope fibers. As the gun is prepared to fire the cloth or paper cartridge of gunpowder, generally one third the weight of the ball shot, it is pushed a short way into the muzzle followed by a wad. Then the wooden rammer pushes both all the way into the barrel. After the shot is loaded, a second wad is rammed to form a tight explosive package as well as to keep the ball from sliding out as the ship pitches and rolls.

CHAIN SHOT, CANNON PROJECTILE
Padstow Shipwreck Museum, Padstow, Cornwall
Cast iron. Each cylinder is 14cm. in diameter.

This projectile was recovered from the undersea wreck site of the East Indiaman *Admiral Gardner*. It is virtually identical to the chain shot that was in general use by the Royal Navy. This example fit snugly into the smooth bore of a 24-pounder.

The shot would be timed with the roll of the ship to be directed not at the hull but above decks at the sails, masts and rope rigging, where the most damage could be done.

FLEXIBLE RAMMER *and* SPONGE
Chatham Historic Dockyard Museum, Chatham, Kent
95mm. in diameter

This is a flexible rammer and sponge for HMS *Invincible*'s 9-pound gun. This combination tool was alternately used to ram home the cartridge and shot in loading and then wet-sponge the bore of the gun after it had been fired, before reloading.

The "sponge" was usually sheepskin that would have covered the wood on the narrow end in this example. The same tools also existed at opposite ends of a long wooden stave, but the advantage of this flexible method was that ramming and sponging could be carried out with the gunport closed or with the gun "run in." In battle, a member of the gun crew often had to sit out on the sill of the gunport to access the gun's muzzle where he could be targeted by small arms. This tool (the rope would ordinarily have been quite rigid) allowed him a measure of safety inside.

CANNON PROJECTILE
Padstow Shipwreck Museum, Padstow, Cornwall
30cm. long

This very unusual expanding shot was recovered from the *Admiral Gardner*, which was lost in 1809. Often the arms on East Indiamen were experimental or weapons that were not yet widely used in the Royal Navy. The carronade, for example, was put into service on some East Indiamen shortly after it was developed.

This cast-iron device would have originally had a total of four such pieces with their rings entwined. The heavy end pieces would nest together to form a cylinder that corresponded to the bore of the cannon. When the contraption was fired from the muzzle of the gun with a bore of 15 centimeters, it would spring open and cartwheel through the air with a new diameter of 60 centimeters. This, of course, greatly increased the chance that it would slash away mast, sail, rigging or whatever should be in its path. To sailors who have said that nothing can describe the sound of a cannonball whizzing past your head, this must have sounded like the "hammers of hell."

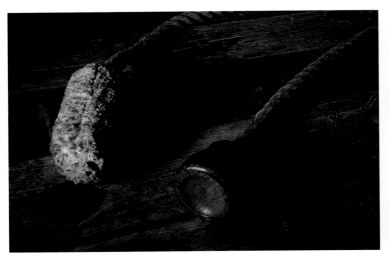

FLEXIBLE RAMMER and SHEEPSKIN "SPONGE", upper left
HMS *Victory*, Portsmouth, Hampshire
The wooden end is 11cm. in diameter.
Wood, rope and sheepskin.

The fact that the front surface of the rammer is cupped would indicate that this is from a later period. Most eighteenth century examples are either flat or drilled completely through for insertion of a round stave.

COPPER VENT HOLE, lower left
Chatham Ordnance Gallery
Chatham Historic Dockyard, Chatham, Kent
The gun's full length is 270cm.

This is a view from behind an 18-pounder of Blomefield design. When a gun has seen a lot of service and fired repeatedly, the touch hole, or vent, gets enlarged. The hole here is in a copper plug. The entire plug can be replaced, containing a hole of the correct size.

VENT HOLE on 9-POUNDER, upper right
Manufactured by the Carron Company of Falkirk, Scotland.
The hole is 4mm.

The powder charge is rammed all the way back into the gun as one of the crew is holding a thin wire probe into the vent hole to feel that the powder cartridge is fully seated. When he can feel it he says: "home." Then he can prick open the cartridge and insert a quill fuse. A small quantity of additional powder is puddled at the hollow "breech block" behind the hole. The gun is now loaded, fused and primed.

RAMMER HEADS, lower right
Chatham Historic Dockyard Museum, Chatham, Kent

These rammer heads show the size of the bore of HMS *Invincible*'s largest guns. The head at left, which serves the 24-pounder, is 13cm. in diameter. The head on the right, which fit the 32-pounder, is 15cm. in diameter. These could be fitted to a stave or rigged as a flexible rammer.

WORM
Chatham Ordnance Gallery
Chatham Historic Dockyard Museum, Chatham, Kent
The coil is 12cm. in diameter.

This "worm" is one of the basic gunnery tools for muzzle-loading cannons. After the cannon is fired, the worm is used to extract any pieces of the cartridge, cinders or unburned powder. This one is a replica of the 32-pounder, built by the Chatham Ordnance Gallery. It is forged iron mounted on a 10-foot ash stave with the "sponge" on the opposite end.

HANDSPIKES
HMS *Trincomalee*, Hartlepool, Teesside
180cm. long

One of these sturdy wooden levers would be used to aim the gun. They were also referred to as "Samson's bar" or a "crow." When the gun lurches back in recoil after it has been fired it must be reloaded and run back out for the next shot. Aiming a 2-ton gun from a rolling, pitching ship at a target that is another vessel also pitching and rolling calls for a practiced crew. Accuracy was frequently the result of a last-second nudge with the spike. It could be used to trip the gun carriage left or right, or as a lever to incline the barrel up or down.

GRAPE SHOT
Chatham Historic Dockyard Museum,
Chatham, Kent

These cast-iron balls are certainly larger than a grape;
slightly smaller than a tennis ball would be a closer
reference. They were often loaded into the great guns
as a parcel of nine balls, tightly stacked in three layers
of three and bound in a cloth bag. They were used as
anti-personnel weapons.

SHOT GARLANDS on HMS WARRIOR
Portsmouth, Hampshire

HMS *Warrior* is a ship from a later era but has features that
were typical of Nelson's time. A supply of shot was kept at
hand near each gun, sometimes painted or greased, ready
for action. Reserves were kept in the lower hold where
they would, likely, become scaled with rust. Chipping of
shot so it could be loaded smoothly was a constant chore
before and after battle. Many captains felt that the fully
armed warship should have 60 cannonballs for each gun
that she carried.

BREECHING ROPES
HMS *Warrior*
HM Naval Base, Portsmouth, Hampshire
17cm. circumference

These were used to secure the gun and its carriage to the ship's side. Since the deck is open to the weather the rope has been tarred. The ends have been combed out and spliced back on themselves.

VIEW from INSIDE the GUNPORT
HMS *Victory*, HM Naval Base, Portsmouth, Hampshire

This gun is more or less ceremonially run out for display purpose. If it were rigged for action the breeching rope would be secured from the rear of the gun to a ring on either side of the gunport. This would check the recoil after the gun is fired at a point where the crew could quickly prepare it to fire again. A second tackle would be attached to the gun carriage and made fast to rings at the port. A third set could be rigged from the rear of the carriage to rings in the deck to pull the gun in manually.

The inside frame of the gunport, painted red, shows the thickness of oak protecting the men from enemy fire, less than a foot at this point. This afforded a measure of protection from smaller arms, but a 32-pounder was capable of penetrating two feet of seasoned oak.

WOODEN VENT STOPPER for CANNON
Chatham Historic Dockyard Museum, Chatham, Kent
4.5cm. long. Recovered from HMS *Invincible*.

The vent hole on the top of a cannon is just a few centimeters long and leads directly to the chamber where the powder charge explodes. The diameter of the vent is just large enough to accept a fuse that was sometimes made from a hollow swan or goose quill lined with powder. Needless to say, when the main charge was touched off, sending the ball on its way, there was a responding backfire sending a jet of hot gas and flame up the vent hole.

After the gun was fired, the gun crew inserted the "worm" into the barrel to clean out any smoldering bits of powder or cartridge, and then the wet sponge extinguished any remaining sparks and cooled down the barrel. The vent stopper would be in place during both of these operations. It prevented the tools inserted into the muzzle from acting as a piston, fouling the vent or sucking air into the vent, igniting glowing debris and possibly setting off unburned powder.

CARTRIDGE BOX
HMS *Invincible*, Chatham Historic Dockyard Museum
Chatham, Kent
48cm. tall

To minimize the risk of accidental explosion, each of the seventy-four guns on HMS *Invincible* would be resupplied with powder only as needed. One member of each gun crew was assigned to make runs to the powder handling rooms below deck. Since the route often involved narrow passage-ways, rope ladders and other obstacles, boys were often given the duty and called "powder monkeys."

This container was fashioned from a single piece of very light poplar wood with the tight fitting cover made of elm.

The traffic of these boys racing to and fro was very care-fully orchestrated. The container would hold no more than two or three bags of powder pre-measured for each type of gun plus the required wads. It was designed originally with a strong cotton twine that attached to the sides and was threaded through holes in the lid so that the cover would stay attached. At some point, the admiralty was concerned that in bloody combat loose gunpowder could stick to the cotton lanyard, effectively turning it into a fuse. It was replaced with a leather thong.

TOMPION
HMS *Invincible*, Chatham Historic Dockyard Museum
Chatham, Kent
13cm. diameter

In times of war cannon were often kept loaded and shotted at all times. The tight-fitting wooden plug sealed up the muzzle and kept out rain, spray and damp.

FELT PURSE with SLOW MATCH
Chatham Historic Dockyard Museum, Chatham, Kent
12.5cm. diameter

The purse is shown as it was recovered from the wrecked HMS *Invincible*. The felt pouch contains a coil of "slow match," which could be cut to length as needed. It was usually a cotton twine impregnated with sulfur and resin. A section of slow match would be held at the end of a wooden rod, called a lin-stock, and lighted to provide a slow-burning ember to ignite the charge on the great guns.

GUNS on HMS VICTORY
HM Naval Base, Portsmouth, Hampshire

In port or in non-hostile situations the gunports could be opened and the guns "run out," thus providing light, air circulation and additional deck space for the hundreds of men who slept, ate and worked in these cramped quarters.

At left, we see the three-gun-deck potential of HMS *Victory*. In rough sea conditions it would sometimes be necessary to shut the lower gunports to keep from shipping water. The checkerboard arrangement spread the tremendous weight of the guns more evenly among the ship's structural timbers. The bold graphic design was preferred by Nelson. It would announce the ship's presence at a great distance.

Borough of Portsmouth } **Whereas** the Right Honourable the Lords Commissioners of the Admiralty having been pleased to accept of the Offer made to them in pursuance of the unanimous Resolutions of the Mayor and Aldermen of the said Borough at a Meeting held at the Guildhall on the seventeenth Day of May last of one hundred Pounds from the Funds of the Corporation to be paid in Addition to His Majesty's Royal Bounty to the first hundred Seamen that should enter for any of His Majesty's Ships at this Port **Now therefore** We the Mayor and Major part of the Aldermen *whose Hands are hereunto set* do hereby consent order and direct that Mr Richard White the Chamberlain shall advance and pay out of the Corporation Fund the said Sum of one hundred Pounds in the Proportion of one Pound to each of such Seamen who shall so enter into His Majesty's Service as the same shall from Time to Time be applied for Witness our Hands this seventh Day of June // one thousand eight hundred and three

S Hazzlee Mayor.

Jn Godwin

Tho White

John Adam Carter

John Carter

Wm Goldson

Borough of Portsmouth } We, the Mayor Aldermen consent or White the the Corporation Pounds to the Constable Compensation lately received the Theatre the Surgeon on account this 7th D

H Ga Jn G

Tho White

John C

Wm Goldson

John Adam

Documents and Letters

ENTRY CONCERNING ONE-POUND BOUNTY
Portsmouth City Museum, Portsmouth, Hampshire

The mayor and the aldermen voted to appropriate 100 pounds sterling from the town's treasury to be provided as a bounty "in addition to His Majesty's Royal Bounty" in the amount of one pound to each of "the first 100 seamen that should enter for any of His Majesty's Ships at this Port. June 7, 1803."

This would indicate that just sixteen months before the great battle at Trafalgar it was not easy to find enough men to crew the Royal Navy ships. One can almost sense the mixture of patriotism and alarm at the French menace that moved the borough authorities to open their coffers to help the English cause.

SAILOR'S LETTER
To HIS WIFE
Portsmouth City Museum
Portsmouth, Hampshire

"My dear if you come to Portsmouth let me know where to direct to you and as soon as I know my Captain I will send something to assist you— I am very well at present.

So no more at present
From your loving husband

John Curtase
Till Death"

PIGMENT BARREL
Chatham Historic Dockyard
Museum, Chatham, Kent
24cm. long, 5cm. diameter

One of several small barrels found on HMS *Invincible*. It is built of five pine staves, tightly fitted and wrapped with four bamboo hoops. Ends would have had wooden plugs, or "heads." Several of these little barrels contained a substance that, when mixed with water, formed ink. Others contained fine sand used for blotting.

Dr Wife Spithead Jan.y 19.th 1800

This comes with my kind
love to you, hoping these few
lines will find you in good
health, as this leaves me at present.
I thank God for it, I was draughted
this day from the Royal
William to the Prostyte Frigate
which will sail clevry soon, her
Destination is not know yet, but I
believe she is going to the west Indies
if so, I will let you know of it as soon
as possible, Dr Wife please to write
as soon as possible and let me know
how the child Comes on — So no
at present from your ever loving husband
till Death — Jn.o Carter

SAILOR'S LETTER to His WIFE
Portsmouth City Museum
Portsmouth, Hampshire

"Spithead, January 19, 1800
Dear Wife,
This comes with my kind love to you, hoping these few lines will find you in good health, as this leaves me at present. Thank God for it. I was draughted this day from the Royal William to the Prostyte Frigate which will sail very soon, her destination is not know (sic) yet, but I believe she is going to the West Indies if so, I will let you know of it as soon as possible. Dear wife please to write as soon as possible and let me know how the child comes on—so no more at present from your ever loving husband till Death.
        —Jno [Jonathan] Carter"

Obviously, a sailor could send and receive mail more easily in port than at sea. Relaying rumors of assignments, awaiting pay, fighting loneliness and boredom and thinking of home, he waits to ship out.

Small Arms

WILLIAMSON BLUNDERBUSS PISTOL
Hartlepool Historic Quay Museum, Hartlepool, Teesside
Barrel 11cm., overall length 17cm.

The jaws of the "cock," or hammer, grip a small piece of flint stone with a leather patch wrapped around one end to secure it. The frizzen, the flap of hardened steel that the flint will strike, is shown swung open, revealing the "pan," which must be primed with a small amount of powder.

The brass barrel is octagonal at the breech end and takes on a round cannon shape closer to the muzzle.

This is a simple gun with few moving parts and almost devoid of decoration. Although it fired a single shot and its accuracy could not be trusted beyond a few paces, it was certainly deadly in point-blank, hand-to-hand fighting.

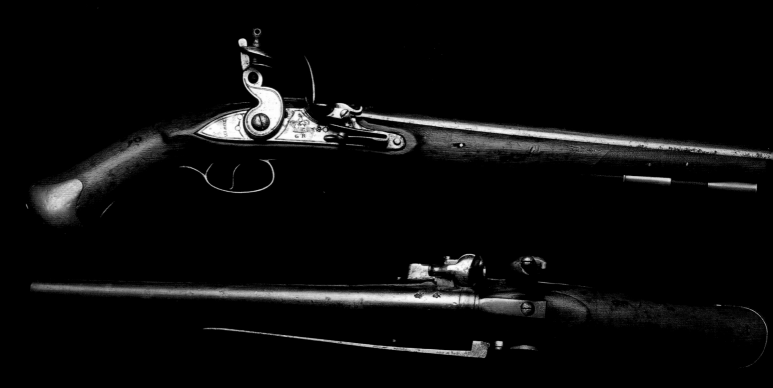

SEA SERVICE PISTOL
Hartlepool Historic Quay Museum, Hartlepool, Teesside
Barrel 35cm., overall length 50cm.

The flintlock sea service pistol originates from about 1810.
This classic form has a full wooden stock that extends to
the muzzle and a heavy brass "skullcrusher" buttcap.

The gun has a steel barrel and the top view shows a belt
hook. Sometimes the pistol was hooked into a sash around
the waist, pirate style.

NOCK BAYONET BLUNDERBUSS PISTOL
Hartlepool Historic Quay Museum, Hartlepool, Teesside
Barrel 21cm., overall length excluding bayonet 29cm.

This brass barreled flintlock blunderbuss pistol was made by
Henry Nock of London, 1760-1810, one of the most famous
London gunsmiths. It incorporates a locking spring bayonet,
which acted as a second line of defense. The bayonet flicks
into place when the trigger guard is pulled. The ramrod can
be seen mounted along the gun's barrel.

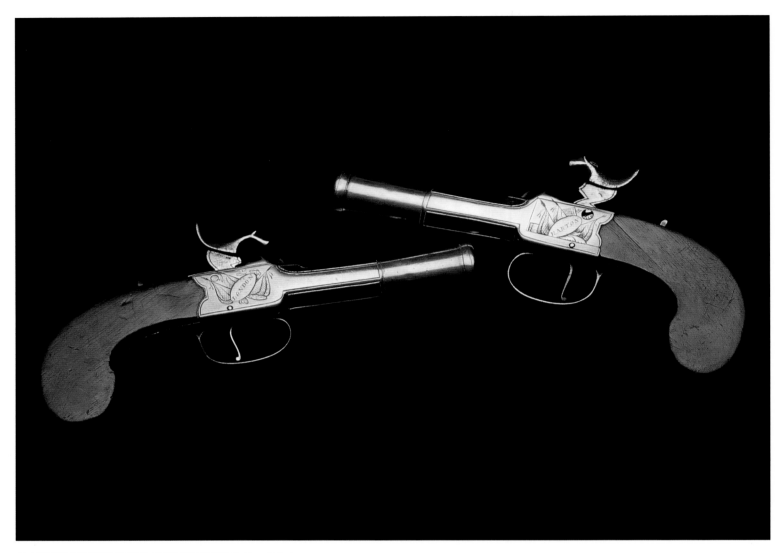

BARTON BLUNDERBUSS PISTOLS, detail below
Hartlepool Historic Quay Museum, Hartlepool, Teesside
Barrel 12cm., overall length 18.5cm.

The barrels are of a bronze gun metal rather than brass, and
have been converted from flintlock to percussion. Carrying a
pair of these pistols was the only sure way to get two shots off
rapidly. The barrel and side plate are formed as a single piece.

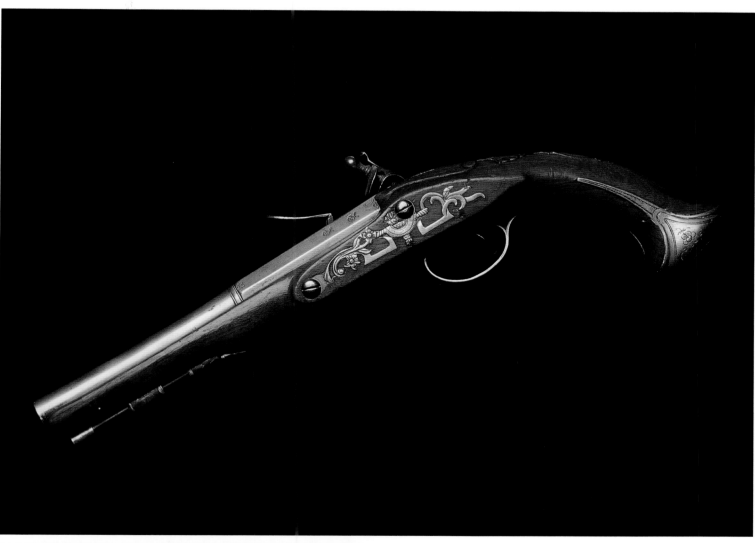

GABBITAS PISTOL

Hartlepool Historic Quay Museum, hartlepool, Teesside
Barrel is 20cm., overall length 36cm.

The gunsmith Gabbitas worked in Bristol in the final quarter
of the eighteenth century, about 1776. This was a gentleman's
gun. The breech of the barrel is octagonal and rounded
towards the flared muzzle. In addition to the very fancy brass
inlay in the stock, there is subtle floral engraving and tooling
on the barrel as well as the buttcap.

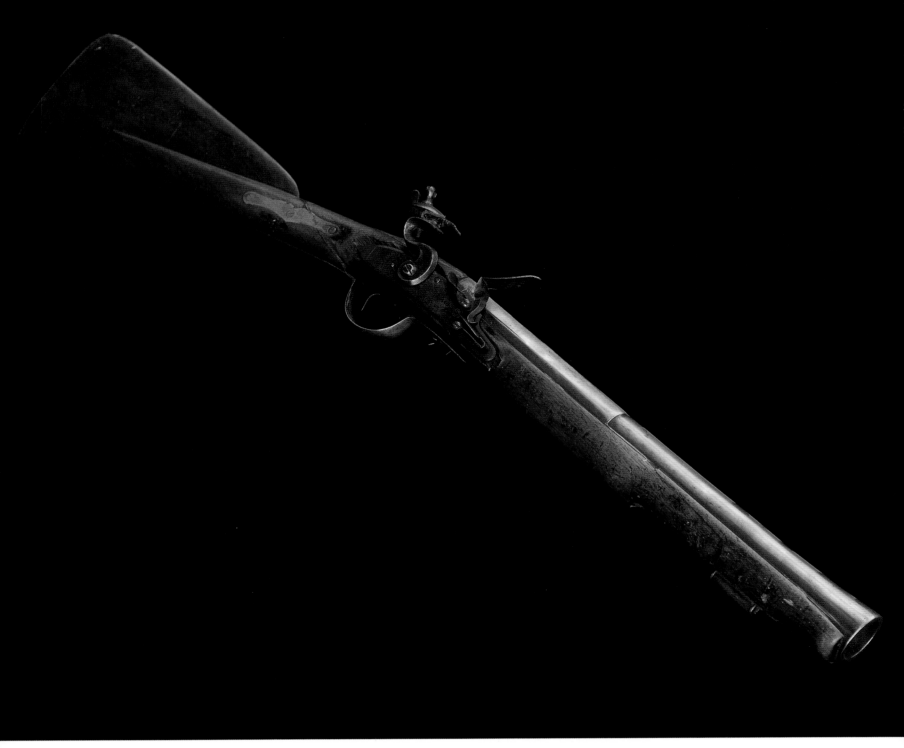

SEA SERVICE BLUNDERBUSS
Hartlepool Historic Quay Museum, Hartlepool, Teesside
Barrel 40cm., overall length 81cm.

The sea service blunderbuss was a simple, mass-produced gun that could be issued to boarding parties or to fight back such an attempt by the enemy. The barrel was made of a very hard brass that we would probably categorize as bronze.

The lock plate (above) is devoid of decoration but stamped with several identifying marks: "Wheeler" is the gunmaker, the crown and letters "GR," for King George, mark it as government property, and the arrow to the right of the crown is a form of the broad arrow, indicating that the barrel had been "proved" or test fired to government satisfaction.

Behind the lockplate can be seen a brass plate that is screwed into the stock to repair a break. After the single shot was fired the gun was often thrown or used as a club.

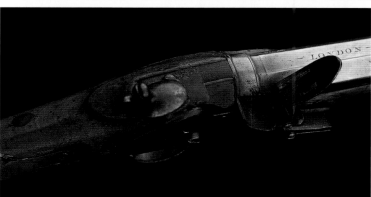

The frizzen (left) shows scratch marks where the flint has pre-viously made contact. When the two make contact, the spring pops the frizzen back and allows the shower of sparks to be driven into the powder that has been "primed" into the pan below. The chain reaction is intended to carry the spark through the tiny vent hole at the side of the pan, setting off the main charge of powder that was muzzle-loaded.

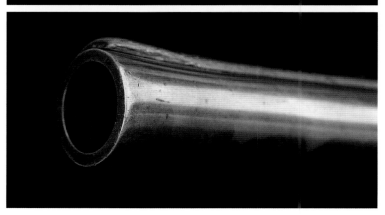

The fact that the muzzle is flared out in a bell shape (below left) did not, as some would expect, scatter the shot in a wider pattern, but made it easier to load the muzzle with small bits of lead, gravel or other projectiles.

PISTOL by BOND
Hartlepool Historic Quay Museum, Hartlepool, Teesside
Barrel 18cm., overall length 33cm.

The Bond family were celebrated gunsmiths to military officers from 1768 to 1879. The steel lock and trigger guard decorated with the pineapple finial dates this flintlock gun between 1790 and 1810. The octagonal barrel bears a "London" proof-mark engraved in script on the top flat. The stock is a single piece of wood extending all the way to the muzzle.

The back side of the one-piece stock, shown on the opposite page, allows us to see that the maker's carving provides a little extra heft and thickness near the area that is hollowed out to accommodate the trigger mechanism. Lower right shows engraved detail from the barrel top and lock plate.

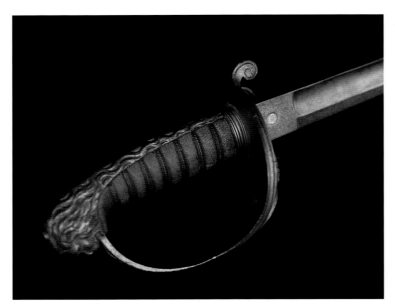

DOCKYARD SWORD, handle detail
Greenwich Borough Museum, Plumstead, London
Blade 795mm; overall length 945mm.

The pommel is a lion's head. The lion's mouth holds the "D" handle knuckle-guard. The dogfish skin grip is wrapped with bronze wire. The maker's mark reads, "Henry Wilkinson of Pall Mall," London. It was the sword of the Woolwich Dockyard Battalion.

BOARDING AX
Hull Maritime Museum, Queen Victoria Square
Kingston-upon-Hull
38.5cm. long

This boarding ax or tomahawk from HMS *Victory* has a one-piece iron head with wooden handle and a diamond-shaped metal plate that reads "R3." It was used not only as a weapon but also to cut away enemy rigging. A well-directed chop could disable the steering, bring down a sail, weaken mast supports, ruin gun tackle or otherwise impede the enemy's ability to fight and maneuver.

FLINTLOCK PISTOLS
Morris Maritime Museum, Penzance, Cornwall
Larger pistol 37.5cm. overall length, smaller pistol 29cm.

The smaller pistol has a steel barrel, steel ramrod and brass buttcap. Faint markings can be seen on the lock plate indicating "Tower," "GR" Royal Crown and the broad arrow proofmark.

The larger pistol has a steel barrel with a wooden ramrod. It is unusual in that it has a front sight, a brass blade, to improve, perhaps, the accuracy of this simple weapon.

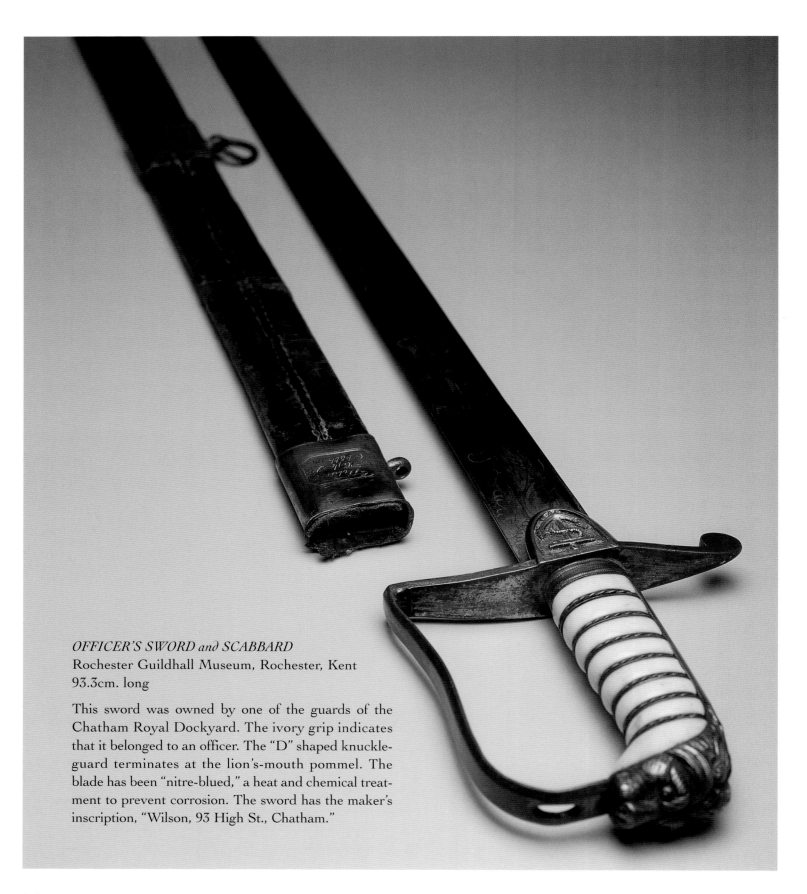

OFFICER'S SWORD and SCABBARD
Rochester Guildhall Museum, Rochester, Kent
93.3cm. long

This sword was owned by one of the guards of the Chatham Royal Dockyard. The ivory grip indicates that it belonged to an officer. The "D" shaped knuckle-guard terminates at the lion's-mouth pommel. The blade has been "nitre-blued," a heat and chemical treatment to prevent corrosion. The sword has the maker's inscription, "Wilson, 93 High St., Chatham."

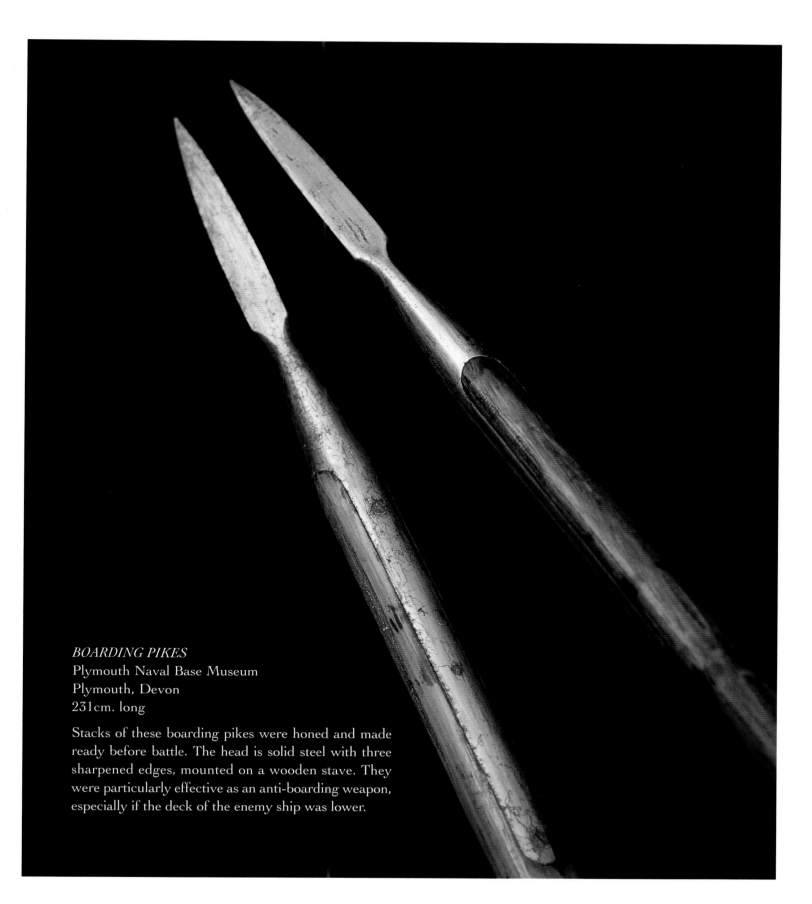

BOARDING PIKES
Plymouth Naval Base Museum
Plymouth, Devon
231cm. long

Stacks of these boarding pikes were honed and made ready before battle. The head is solid steel with three sharpened edges, mounted on a wooden stave. They were particularly effective as an anti-boarding weapon, especially if the deck of the enemy ship was lower.

GRENADE with WOODEN FUSE
Royal Marines Museum, Southsea, Hampshire
7cm. diameter

This hollow cast-iron ball was filled with about three ounces of gunpowder and fitted with the wooden fuse shown. It was lighted and thrown.

A detachment of marines was assigned to many warships. They would target men on the enemy ships with small arms fire. In close action they would take positions up in the rigging where they could shoot downward or throw these deadly anti-personnel weapons among the crew of the enemy ship alongside.

HAND GRENADE with BEECHWOOD FUSE
Chatham Historic Dockyard Museum
Chatham, Kent
11cm. diameter

This larger grenade was recovered from the HMS *Invincible* with the beechwood fuse intact. These weapons were carefully fabricated with a double linen or canvas seal around the fuse, wrapped wth twine and waterproofed with sealing wax. The burn rate of the fuse varied and made this a risky missile.

WOODEN CARTRIDGE HOLDER
Recovered from HMS *Invincible*.
Chatham Historic Dockyard Museum, Chatham, Kent
25cm. across

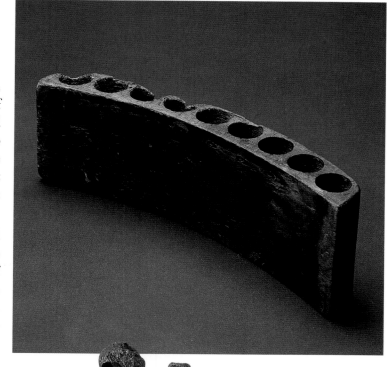

To speed up the rate of fire for muzzle-loading muskets, cartridges were prepared by wrapping measured amounts of gunpowder in waxed or greased cartridge paper with the lead shot tied in at one end. The entire parcel could be rammed into the barrel. This would leave the marksman only to pierce the paper with a toothpick-like vent pricker, pour a small amount of gunpowder into the priming pan, cock the hammer back, aim and fire.

There was also a technique whereby the marksman would break open the prepared cartridge with his teeth and hold the lead ball in his mouth. He would prime the pan with a bit of powder from the torn cartridge and push the remainder into the barrel. He would then spit the ball into the barrel. This would increase the rate of fire by eliminating the need to prime from a separate powder horn and prick open the rammed cartridge.

FLINTLOCK
Chatham Historic Dockyard Museum,
Chatham, Kent
12cm. across

This lock recovered from HMS *Invincible* utilizes a mechanism that could be used to fire a musket, pistol or cannon.

Marksmen had to be trained not to flinch at the initial powder spark and spoil their aim. If this initial spark failed to set off the main charge it was merely a "flash in the pan."

Discipline

CAT-O'-NINE-TAILS
Plymouth Naval Base Museum, Plymouth, Devon
65cm. long

Discipline was harsh in the Royal Navy of the late eighteenth century. "Starting" was usually an impromptu whack with a cane, rod or length of rope. It was often meted out by the bosun's mate to any sailor who was deemed to be lazy, insolent or to have committed almost any infraction. Even a midshipman, possibly as young as ten years old, could give the command: "Start that man!"

Flogging offenses were determined by the captain, and it was generally the rule that only up to a dozen lashes could be given without a formal court-martial. All hands were summoned on deck to witness the punishment. The man was usually bound hand and foot to a wooden ship's grating that had been mounted vertically, and the lashes were delivered across his bare back. The ship's surgeon would often rub salt into the torn flesh to prevent infection. For more severe punishment, for instance forty lashes, the blows would be administered by a succession of men, so that each blow would be of full intensity.

There are stories that insist that the condemned man was forced to plait his own "cat" to specific dimensions, and that it would be used only once and thrown overboard. But it is also recorded that the bosun's mate kept his personal cat in a red cloth bag, and that the crew knew that a flogging was imminent if they went past the mate's duty station and saw that "the cat was out of the bag." It is also thought that the notion of very confined space gives us the expression "not enough room to swing a cat."

MINIATURE GUILLOTINE
Hartlepool Historic Quay Museum, Hartlepool, Teesside
30cm. tall

This witty little guillotine toy is made of mutton bones that have been shaped, stained and fitted together. It shows soldiers in attendance at the execution of a young woman. It features a working blade and rope trigger, removable head and catching basket.

There was no notion of humane treatment of prisoners in the Napoleonic Era; even providing food was not a given. Prisoners were frequently forced to work to earn their bread. Picking the strands of old rope apart to make oakum for caulking was one prison occupation. In Devon, prisoners of war were used to build Dartmoor Prison, where they themselves would soon be held.

The men became very resourceful at creating objects for sale to their captors. They often used the simplest material imaginable: straw, meat bones or even their own hair.

BONE "CASKET," *above*
Hartlepool Historic Quay Museum, Hartlepool, Teesside
25cm. across

This finely decorated covered box is made from strips of mutton bone by Napoleonic prisoners of war.

The generic name for the tremendous variety of pieces such as this is "Soup Bone Art" or "French Prisoner Art." However, the prison population at that time included large numbers of Americans, Spaniards, Danes and Swedes.

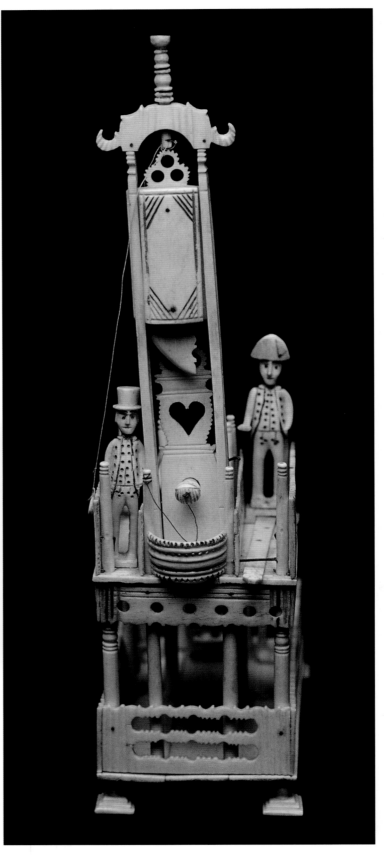

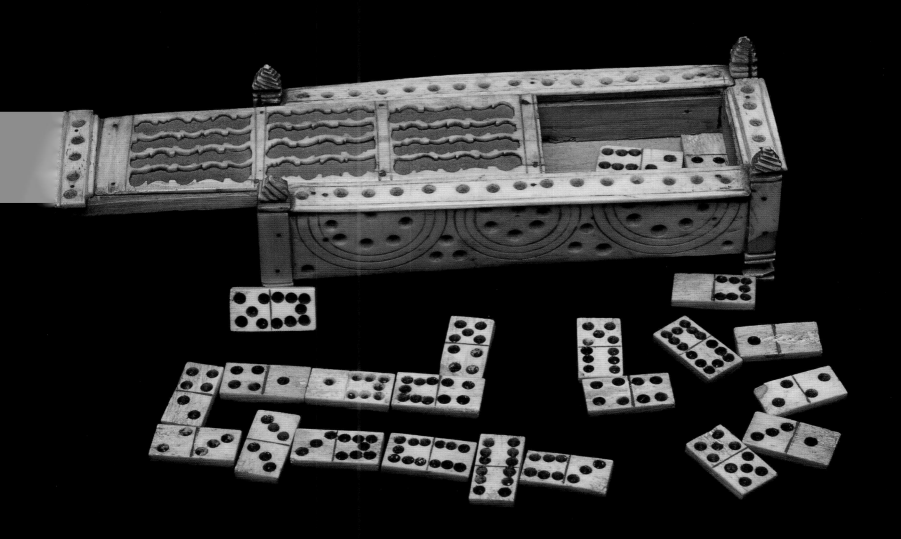

DOMINO SET
Hartlepool Historic Quay Museum, Hartlepool, Teesside
Box is 20cm. across

This domino set was made by a French prisoner of war from mutton bones. The maker has created pieces with an extra dot, a "seven," in order to extend the game and make it last longer.

BLACK JACK–STYLE COSH
Hartlepool Historic Quay Museum, Hartlepool, Teesside
30cm. at full length

This weapon is made using a sailing man's skills with eye-spliced rope and stitched leather weighted with lead and sand. It is painful to think of it in the hands of a press-gang.

These predatory gangs, looking for able men for duty on war-ships, were not supposed to be armed with swords or pistols. They needed the pressed men uninjured and fit for work.

TOMBSTONE
Graveyard in St. Ives, Cornwall

Thomas Williams and his cousin, John Tregarthen Short, both from Cornwall, and about seventeen years old, didn't wish to be pressed into the Royal Navy, so they went to sea working on their uncle's merchant boat. They were soon seized by the French and spent ten years in prison in France.

In spite of this, they came home to St. Ives and both lived long and full lives. Short founded a school of navigation.

Miscellaneous and Curiosities

GIMBALED IRON LAMP
Hartlepool Historic Quay Museum, Hartlepool, Teesside
17.5cm. in diameter

Lamps of this design were used on ships from the sixteenth to the nineteenth centuries. When hung by the ring, the candle or oil flame would stay level as the ship pitched and rolled. These same lamps were also used by sheep and cow herders in Rajasthan, India.

HOG BRISTLE DECK BUMPER, *below*
Chatham Historic Dockyard Museum, Chatham, Kent
60cm. long

This deck bumper was used for cleaning the decks and was found in very good condition among HMS *Invincible* artifacts. It is scratched on the back side with the broad arrow.

The perforated brush plate has tapered holes. Hog bristles, both hard and soft, are fastened on the inside by copper wire.

SWEEPING BRUSH, *at right*
Chatham Historic Dockyard Museum, Chatham, Kent
20cm. long

This is smaller and much rougher than the deck bumper. It was used for general deck cleaning on HMS *Invincible*.

BRASS MAHARAJA'S LOCK
Hartlepool Historic Quay Museum, Hartlepool, Teesside
Lock is 26.5cm. long. Largest key is 12.5cm. long.

This lock is solid brass with an internal explosive mechanism. The curious device would probably have seen service on an East Indiaman rather than a Royal Navy vessel.

The lock was armed with a lethal charge of gunpowder that would explode in the hands and face of any thief that attempted to pick it.

SHELL-DECORATED SEWING BASKET
Hartlepool Historic Quay Museum, Hartlepool, Teesside
22cm. across

When a warship was not in action or on blockade duty she was essentially overmanned. The crew had long stretches of idle time. Sailors would sometimes create such labors of love with the simplest of materials.

WARSHIP SNUFF BOX
Hartlepool Historic Quay Museum, Hartlepool, Teesside
12.5cm. long

This snuff box with a hinged lid is carved in a warship design from fruitwood and boxwood.

WARRIOR PENDANT with TASSELS
Hartlepool Historic Quay Museum, Hartlepool, Teesside
14cm. across

This "warrior pendant" is formed from buffalo hide and wild boar tusks and decorated with cowrie shells and seeds. Such were the gifts and souvenirs that sailors brought home from their travels.

WILD BOAR TUSK PENDANT
Hartlepool Historic Quay Museum, Hartlepool, Teesside
12.5cm. across

Among the Naga people of northern Burma this pendant made from the tusks of a wild boar was a symbol worn by a young warrior after taking a human head.

MINIATURE BIBLE and HAND MAGNIFIER
Hartlepool Historic Quay Museum, Hartlepool, Teesside
Book: 4.5cm. high. Boxwood Magnifier: 15cm. long.

One wonders whether the sailor was "packing small" for his one seabag or perhaps hiding his piety from his shipmates.

BOSUN'S PIPE with LANYARD
Greenwich Borough Museum, Plumstead, London
12.5cm. long

The "bosun" (literally "boatswain") was a warrant officer who often acted as a strong arm to prod the men to carry out other officer's orders promptly.

This pipe, or "call," was worn on a lanyard, and its shrill notes were designed to be heard by the crew whether they were aloft or alow. It announced visitors (piped them aboard) and conveyed orders to the crew. This example is marked with the broad arrow.

SAILOR'S KNIVES
Hartlepool Historic Quay Museum, Hartlepool, Teesside
21.5cm. each

The handmade knife below, has a wooden handle inlaid with brass and bone and decorated with twine. The loop is a leather thong. The knife above has a curved horn handle.

Workingmen's knives show off the unique personality of the maker or the owner. If the knife-makers kept these for their own use, it's a fair assumption that their shipmates were eager to place orders for one of their own.

PRICK (PRIQUE) Of TOBACCO
Falmouth Maritime Museum, Falmouth, Cornwall
32cm. long

Tobacco was a regular and very important part of the men's rations. The tobacco leaves were saturated with rum to cure and preserve them, formed into a tight loaf, then rolled in canvas. The parcel was then "served" with wet line into this form, which tightly compressed the loaf. Plugs were sliced up for distribution. The men would usually chew or pipe smoke.

CUSTOMS INSPECTOR'S WALKING STICK
Deal Maritime Museum, Deal, Kent
86cm. overall

This 4-sided steel blade slides away, concealed in a wooden walking stick. It was not a sword but the standard tool-of-the-trade for a customs inspector. Deal was a port with lively smuggling activity, and this probe was for poking into bales, bundles and cargo looking for contraband.

COMMEMORATIVE INLAID BOX
Falmouth Maritime Museum, Falmouth, Cornwall
Lid is 10cm. across.

This inlaid ivory and ebony box commemorates the launch of a warship, probably a "64," in the opinion of the museum curator, as evidenced by the incomplete upper deck. They have knocked away the stocks and she is sliding down the slipway, stern first. Since her masts are not in at this stage, enormous launching flags are flown at those positions. The museum has identified them as: Forward: Union Flag; Foremast: Flag of Admiralty; Mainmast: Royal Standard; Mizzenmast: White Ensign; Aft: Union Flag.

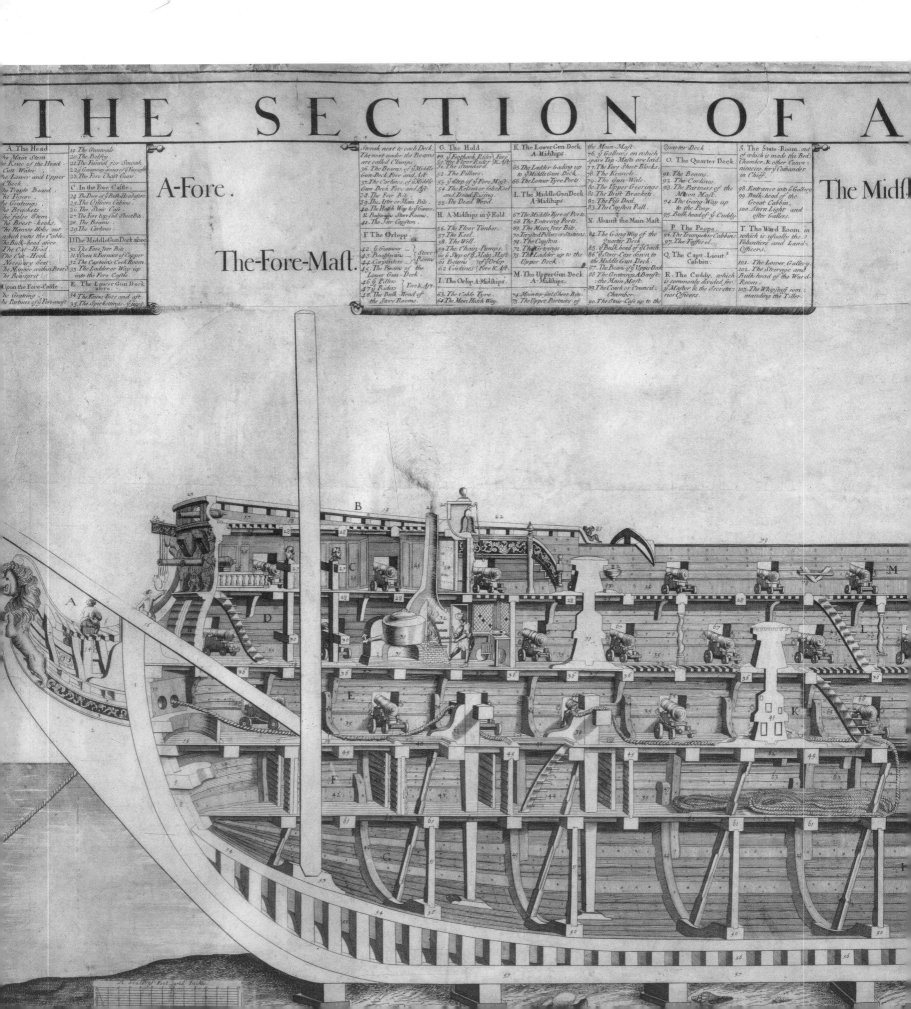

THE SECTION OF A

A-Fore.

The-Fore-Maft.

The Midf...

A. The Head.
The Main Stern.
The Knee of the Head.
Cutt Water.
Check.
The Trayle Board.
The Figure.
The Brackets.
The Falfe Stem.
The Brest-hooks.
The Hawse Holes out which runs the Cable.
The Cat-Hook.
The Cat-Hook.
Necessary Seat.
The Manger within Board.
The Bowsprit.

Upon the Fore-Caftle.
The Grating.
The Partners of y Fore-maft.

19. The Gunwale.
20. The Belfry.
21. The Funnel for Smoak.
22. y Grimstow aboue of y Forecastle.
23. The Fore Chast Guns.

C. In the Fore Caftle.
24. The Door of y Bulk-head afore.
25. The Officers Cabins.
26. The Stair Case.
27. The Fore top sail Sheet Bitt.
28. The Beams.
29. The Carlines.

D. The Middle Gun Deck aboue.
30. The Fore Jeer Bits.
31. Ouen & Furnace of Copper.
32. The Captain's Cook Room.
33. The Ladder or Way up into the Fore Caftle.

E. The Lower Gun Deck afore.
34. The Knees Fore and aft.
35. The Spirketting of y...

Sweak next to each Deck. The next under the Beams are called Clamps.
36. The Beams, of y Middle Gun-Deck Fore and Aft.
37. The Carlines of y Middle Gun-Deck Fore and Aft.
38. The Jeer Bitt.
39. The After or Main Bitt.
40. The Hatch Way to y Gunn & Boatswains Store Rooms.
41. The Jeer Capstan.

F. The Orlopp.
42. y Gunners ——
43. Boatswains —— Store
44. Carpenters —— Rooms
45. The Beams of the Lower Gun-Deck.
46. y Pillers.
47. y Rudes — Fore & Aft.
48. The Bulk-Head of the Store Rooms.

G. The Hold.
49. y Foothook Rider Fore.
50. The y Floor Rider & Aft.
51. The Standard.
52. The Pillars.
53. y Step of y Fore Maft.
54. The Relson or y y Keel and Dead Rasing.
55. The Dead Wood.

H. A-Midships in y Hold.
56. The Floor Timber.
57. The Keel.
58. The Well.
59. The Chain-Pumps.
60. y Step of y Main Maft.
61. Beams y of y Orlop.
62. Carlines Fore & Aft.

I. The Orlop A-Midships.
63. The Cable Tyre.
64. The Main Hatch Way.

K. The Lower Gun-Deck A-Midships.
65. The Ladder leading up to y Middle Gun-Deck.
66. The Lower Tyre Ports.

L. The Middle Gun-Deck A-Midships.
67. The Middle Tyre of Ports.
68. The Entering Ports.
69. The Main Jeer Bitt.
70. Twisted Pillars or Stations.
71. The Capstan.
72. The Gratings.
73. The Ladder up to the Upper Deck.

M. The Upper Gun-Deck A-Midships.
74. Main top-sails Sheet Bits.
75. The Upper Partners of the Main-Maft.
76. y Gallows on which y spare Top-Mafts are laid.
77. The Fore Sheet Blocks.
78. The Kennels.
79. The Gun-Wale.
80. The Upper Geerings.
81. The Drift Brackets.
82. The Fish Deal.
83. The Capston Pall.

N. Abauft the Main-Maft.
84. The Gang Way of the Quarter Deck.
85. y Bulk-head of y Coach.
86. y Stair-Case down to the Middle Gun Deck.
87. The Beams of y Upper Deck.
88. The Grating A Baust the Main Mast.
89. The Coach or Council Chamber.
90. The Stair-Case up to the Quarter Deck.

O. The Quarter Deck.
91. The Beams.
92. The Carlines.
93. The Partners of the Mizen Maft.
94. The Gang-Way up to the Poop.
95. Bulk-head of y Cuddy.

P. The Poope.
96. The Trumpeters Cabbins.
97. The Tafferel.

Q. The Capt-Lieut.s Cabbin.

R. The Cuddy, which is commonly divided for y Master & the Secreteries Officers.

S. The State-Room, out of which is made the Bed: Chamber, & other Conve: niences for y Comander in Chief.

T. The Ward Room, in which is usually the Volluntiers and Land Officers.

98. Entrance into y Gallery.
99. Bulk-head of the Great Cabbin.
100. Stern Light and after Gallers.
101. The Lower Gallery.
102. The Steerage and Bulk-head of the War d-Room.
103. The Whipstaff com-manding the Tiller.

A Scale of Feet and Inches.